RETRIEVAL PRACTICE

Research & Resources
for every classroom

KATE JONES

First Published 2019

by John Catt Educational Ltd,
15 Riduna Park, Melton, Woodbridge, Suffolk IP12 1QT
01394 389850
enquiries@johncatt.com
www.johncatt.com

Tel: +44 (0) 1394 389850
Fax: +44 (0) 1394 386893
Email: enquiries@johncatt.com
Website: www.johncatt.com

ISBN: 978 1 912906 58 1

Set and designed by John Catt Educational Limited

Dedicated to Mark Duncan and his family Stella, Ian, Louise and Hiba.
An inspiring educator and good friend, taken far too soon.

1 December 1987 – 23 February 2019

PRAISE FOR RETRIEVAL PRACTICE

'Translating evidence into practice, Kate has succeeded in making research a social process for students, teachers and leaders. We all know the importance of "best bets" and what strategies are most likely to work; we also understand that the evidence on retrieval is overwhelming. What the profession is starting to appreciate is that research should supplement teacher expertise, not supplant it. Kate is a practicing teacher and leader, faithfully adopting and intelligently adapting the science to suit her students in her classroom. Kate explains and contextualises the evidence. She gives insights that will be invaluable to students on how to use retrieval practice in their studies, practical advice for teachers for their classroom and implementation advice for senior leaders. If you love to teach and want to be the best teacher you can be, this is the book for you!'

Phil Naylor (@pna1977)
Teacher, senior leader and host of the podcast 'Naylor's Natter'

'I highly recommend Retrieval Practice. *As Kate says, retrieval practice is a low effort, high impact strategy, and it is therefore one that is very worthwhile for all teachers to know more about. As well as running through the fundamental theory in an accessible way, the book highlights many of the broader benefits of retrieval practice, such as improving metacognitive awareness of the learning process among a class, and helping teachers to be more confident about what their class know. And as Kate rightly points out, teachers who report a lack of time to use retrieval should consider that there are few strategies (if any) that result in such benefits for both the durability and transferability of learning. A real strength of the book's approach is the many practical tasks it presents. The diagrams and example worksheets will make such tasks very easy for teachers to understand and implement.'*

Jonathan Firth (@JW_Firth)
Author and Teaching Fellow at the University of Strathclyde, Glasgow

'Kate Jones returns with her second book about retrieval practice for any classroom and once again creates something that perfectly blends educational research with practical ideas for any teacher to implement in their classroom. Kate is a classroom teacher at heart and this comes across in everything she writes. She understands the way classrooms work and I am always in awe at her ideas – it's no different when reading her latest book about retrieval practice. Kate makes me a better teacher through her work and this book is a classic example of just that.'

Tom Rogers (@rogershistory)
TES columnist, Founder and Director of TMIcons and RogersHistory.com

'Kate strikes again, providing us with the very latest in educational research, this time for one of the hottest educational topics at the moment "retrieval practice". Kate effectively removes any doubt that the term is a momentary educational fad and presents quality, consumable educational research that will inspire teachers everywhere.

As is synonymous with Kate's work, she provides excellent resources and ideas which are all low in effort but high in their impact. This book will enthuse every classroom teacher to develop, implement and embed retrieval practice. We have already used the ideas and information from this book in our teaching, CPD sessions, assemblies and parent/carer coffee mornings. We cannot wait to feature it on #BookTalkThursday!'

Matt Walker and Tim Barker (@carpool4school1)
The creators and host of CarPool4School

'Kate Jones is slowly becoming the busy teacher's favourite read. Kate offers concise and accessible summaries of key research relating to retrieval practice before sharing a wide range of ways in which retrieval practice could be effectively embedded into any classroom. This book is an excellent read because Kate generously shares practical ideas that could easily be put to use within the classroom the very next day to benefit pupils' retrieval and retention skills - an area we know is fundamental to learning. Kate's personal, warm style of writing means you come away feeling energised to put her ideas into action. A fantastic middle leader, whose passion for teaching and desire to support others is so evident.'

Freya Odell (@fod3)
Teacher of English at St. George's British International School, Rome

'This is an incredibly timely book, the importance of the working memory and retrieval practices has been highlighted as a core standard in the 2019 Early Careers Framework formulated by the EEF. Whilst there is a growing body of research about the importance of cognitive science related to how students learn, there has not been much written to connect this research to its practical implications for teaching and learning. Interest from teachers into the science of learning has never been greater, but understanding how to apply it in the classroom can be a minefield. Kate has taken apart and translated the research into something that is relatable but most importantly usable.

There is no doubt that this book will fly off the shelves of many CPD libraries; I know that I will be returning to it frequently over the next year as I seek to implement its many practical ideas.'

Dee Saran (@Dee_Saran)
Deputy Headteacher at Dubai College, UAE

'This book helps further illuminate the relationship between theory and how it may walk and breathe in the daily practice of both teachers and learners. It offers clear and readily accessible explanations around retrieval practice as a key facet of memory inquiry and cognitive psychology, helping explain not just what may be effective in terms of practical classroom application, but why it may be effective. It helps further strengthen the co-natural relationship that teaching is learning.'

Mark Healy (@cijane02)
Psychology teacher and Deputy Headteacher at St. Andrew's High School, Coatbridge

CONTENTS

ACKNOWLEDGEMENTS

2019 has been a very year busy for me!

In August I relocated and started a teaching and leadership role at a new school, The British School Al Khubairat in Abu Dhabi. This is a very prestigious, co-educational, non-selective and not-for-profit school. I would like to thank my colleagues for the warm welcome, especially the history and geography departments. Thank you to James McBlane and Nigel Davis for their support and enthusiasm with this book. I am lucky to work with leaders who lead by example and continually promote the message of lifelong learning, therefore I also want to thank Teresa Woulfe, Head of Secondary School and Mark Leppard MBE, Headmaster.

I am very pleased to have had the opportunity to work with the team at John Catt again. Thank you to Alex Sharratt for his enthusiasm, the talented graphic designer Scott James and the kind, hardworking and dedicated editor Meena Ameen. A huge thank you to Tom Sherrington, an educator I greatly admire, for agreeing to write the foreword to this book. Tom has recently authored the very successful book *Rosenshine's Principles in Action* and this book has illustrated how educational books focusing on one key topic, concept or area of research is something that teachers want to read. As you will see he is referenced a lot in this book, thus showing how much I have learned from him!

I am delighted to have been able to include a range of case studies and ideas from leaders and teachers which explore the impact retrieval practice has had. Thank you to all the contributors for taking the time to reflect and contribute to this book. Professionally, I want to show my appreciation and gratitude to Pooja K. Agarwal, Patrice Bain and Blake Harvard. I am very lucky that, despite the distance between us, I have been able to learn so much from Pooja, Patrice and Blake. They are all incredibly supportive of the resources I share and my writing – especially about retrieval practice.

Finally, thanks to all my friends for being there for me, both professionally and personally. As always there are too many people to name and thank. This includes current and former colleagues at all the amazing schools I have had the privilege to work at, in addition to my non-teacher friends that are very supportive in all that I do. Thank you to all the students that I have had the privilege to teach over the years. And, finally, my family: my mother, Heather, and father, Andre, Emily, Paul, Jessica, Jo-anne, Ben, Ella and my Gran Hazel – I am eternally grateful for your kindness and love.

FOREWORD

BY TOM SHERRINGTON

What is retrieval practice and why does it matter? Here's an example. Last year I became frustrated that, despite numerous visits to historical sites and reading various books over the years, my knowledge of Henry VIII's six wives and their life stories was poor. I was forever forgetting the details; I got their names and their respective fates muddled up and I was unable to tell the story with any coherence. Why? I had been relying on fragments of knowledge 'sinking in' somehow but not really engaged in any attempt to retrieve the information in a coherent manner. 'Sinking in' is actually a terrible metaphor for learning. It requires some conscious effort; some determination and, crucially, some practice. I decided to remedy the situation and engaged in a whole process of writing out timelines, re-telling the stories of each wife from memory, checking my recall for accuracy and trying again. Now, after a period of doing this, I've developed a really good sense of the story. When I read more about them, the knowledge seems to stick more easily and my Henry VIII's Six Wives schema is now rich in narrative detail that helps me understand a range of more complex ideas in history, such as the changing link between the church and the state.

Arguably the act of 'practising remembering' is at the very core of what effective learning is about. The more we know, the more we can know. The more we know, the more we can understand. The more often we retrieve knowledge from our vast complex stores of memories in different ways – all those facts, words, ideas, concepts and experiences – the stronger those memories become and the more fluently we can recall them. The more fluent we are in recalling our knowledge, the better placed we are to explore new knowledge, to solve new problems, to engage in debate, to respond to challenges, to understand what we read. The more we know, the more creative we can be.

And yet, forgetting is all too easy. It's probably the most predictable feature of any learning process that lots of students will forget a lot of what their teachers have been trying to teach. It's utterly inevitable but still teachers will often bemoan this fact. 'I can't believe you've forgotten it already!' They'll be disappointed that the new technique, the fascinating word or powerful phrase they discussed at length only last lesson has been only tenuously grasped; it seems to have 'gone in one ear and out the other'. Thankfully, help is at hand.

In my training, I always celebrate the idea that what teachers need to develop is 'evidence-informed wisdom'. We all gain wisdom from experience, learning from our triumphs and disasters, learning from how our students respond to various strategies; learning from teaching the same material to different classes. But I think we should also be seeking out evidence from beyond our experience including from the vast array of studies into teaching and learning and the way the human brain functions. If we can blend evidence from research with the evidence we gather in our classrooms, we won't be feeling our way so much, relying on our hunches; we'll be in a much stronger position to make good decisions. Happily, slowly but surely, I think teaching is becoming a genuinely evidence-informed profession as our access to the wealth of research evidence continues to grow. New blogs, books, conferences and Twitter feeds are helping teachers to access, debate and adapt ideas like never before. It's a truly exciting time to be working in education.

Kate Jones, in my view, is the archetypal contemporary switched-on evidence-engaged teacher. Her books, blog and social media output fizz with enthusiasm and earnest commitment for teaching the subject she loves – History – but also for sharing ideas with other professionals in her school and around the world. She has the authentic voice of a practising teacher, passionate about her subject, determined for her students to succeed but also fascinated by the science of learning and the myriad ways of putting ideas into practice. *Retrieval Practice* pulls so many ideas together starting with a superb exposition of the key ideas from cognitive science then drawing on the experience of teachers across a wide range of subjects to explore their application in real classrooms. If you ever thought that retrieval practice was just a matter of taking a quiz, this book will put you straight. There are so many ideas here, it's really quite remarkable. It's been a real joy to read - a wonderfully written book about a vital subject and I think it's going to be an extremely valuable resource for a lot of teachers.

AN INTRODUCTION TO RETRIEVAL PRACTICE

Has 'retrieval practice' become the latest buzzword in education? That is a concern and frustration felt by many educators I know. There's no denying that it's a very trendy topic at the moment in education – people are tweeting about it, presenting about it at conferences, and now there is even a book completely dedicated to the field.

Whilst it is true that retrieval practice is a term that many educators have only become familiar with in recent years, it is certainly not a fad and, although not completely new, I still consider it to be revolutionary to teaching and learning. It is much more than the latest bandwagon to jump on and hopefully the interest in retrieval practice is not just a passing phase. The key difference between this and other fads that have come and gone in education is that it is supported by vast amounts of research and welcomed by educators as part of their daily teaching practice.

This book was not written with the intention of being dedicated to the field of cognitive psychology (one could be forgiven for thinking that based on the title), but instead it is very much focused on teaching and learning. I am not an academic researcher or cognitive psychologist. I am a classroom teacher and middle leader with a strong interest in this field who has written a book for other teachers who, like myself, simply want to learn *more*. I do reference a lot of research and cognitive psychology, which is necessary when writing about retrieval practice, but I have tried to combine theory and practice from a teacher's perspective.

Retrieval practice refers to the act of recalling learned information from memory (with no or little support) and every time that information is retrieved, or an answer is generated, it changes that original memory to make it stronger.

'Using your memory, shapes your memory' – this is a great description of retrieval from the distinguished and well-respected professor of psychology, Robert Bjork.[1] The retrieval process cements the information

---

1. Gocognitive (2012) 'Robert Bjork – using our memory shapes our memory'. *Youtube* [Video] 12 July. Retrieved from: www.bit.ly/2nAYHgL

in the long-term memory, which should enable that information to become easier to retrieve in the future. Retrieval practice focuses on recalling information from memory as a *powerful learning tool, not an assessment tool*. Therefore, it is regarded as essential classroom practice to support learning with the regular practice of retrieval.

Retrieval practice has previously been referred to by academics and in educational research as the 'testing effect', as naturally the act of recalling information from memory describes the process of a test. Two leading and influential academic researchers in the field of retrieval practice are Henry L. Roediger III and Jeffrey D. Karpicke – both of whom are widely referenced in this book – write that 'testing is a powerful means of improving learning, not just assessing it'.[2]

Testing itself is often used for assessment and judgment rather than as a way to further improve learning, although some tests are designed to do both. It is easy to see why the term 'testing effect' is not as commonplace as retrieval practice due to the negative connotations that come with testing, such as: exam pressure; stress, anxiety and other mental health problems; and, the suggestion that schools are simply exam factories that continually test children and kill creativity, which is simply not true. Retrieval practice is also intended to be low-stakes or no-stakes (meaning the results do not need to be recorded or shared), unlike a high stakes, high-pressure situation such as an external examination. There are many variations of retrieval practice in the classroom, going beyond traditional testing.

In order to fully grasp retrieval practice we need to have a contextual understanding and awareness of the distinction between the different types of memory. This could be a book entirely in itself, but I will just summarise this because often I have wondered, as a teacher, how much of the psychology do I really need to know? Certainly, knowledge of this is important, but there are concerns and potential issues if teachers are expected to become academic experts in cognitive psychology, in addition to experts in our own individual subjects, pedagogy and the wellbeing of students in our care too.

The key areas I believe are highly significant are knowledge of short-term memory (also referred to as 'working memory') and long-term memory. This information is now generally well known amongst teachers as there has been so much discussion of it as of late, but for clarity I will briefly

2. Roediger, H. L. and Karpicke, J. D. (2006) 'Test-Enhanced Learning: Taking Memory Tests Improved Long-Term Retention', *Psychological Science* 17 (3) pp. 249–255.

summarise the key differences between short-term and long-term memory as they are terms I will refer back to throughout. A good starting point is the multi-store model of memory by Richard Atkinson and Richard Shiffrin as shown in the diagram below.[3]

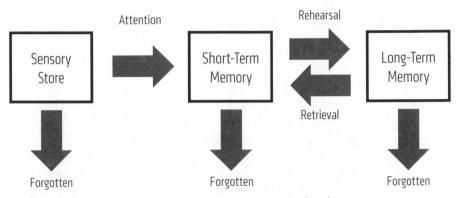

Figure 1 The multi-store model of memory by Atkinson and Shiffrin (1968)

Cognitive psychologists Atkinson and Shiffrin proposed that memory consisted of three stores:

The first is the **sensory store**, where new information is encoded. Subsequently, in the learning process we begin at the attention and encoding stage, but it's important to note that this is not the only stage in the learning process, it's just the beginning. When I started teaching I tended to focus on teaching content and skills, getting that information into students' minds, only for them to try and retrieve it at a much later date, for example an end of unit assessment or exam.

Information is then passed on to the second store: the **short-term memory,** which is also referred to interchangeably as 'working memory', based on further work carried out by Baddeley and Hitch (1974) who believed the original concept of short-term memory with the multi-store model was far too simplistic.[4]

When we encounter new material, the information is stored for a very brief time in our short-term memory. The reason for this is due to the capacity (how much information) and duration (how long we can store it) of our short-term memory, which is very limited. The length of time

3. Atkinson, R. C. and Shiffrin, R. M. (1968) 'Human memory: A proposed system and its control processes', in Spence, K. W. and Spence, J. T. (eds) *The psychology of learning and motivation*. New York, NY: Academic Press, pp. 89-195.
4. Baddeley, A. D. and Hitch, G. (1974) 'Working memory', *Psychology of Learning and Motivation* 8 pp. 47-89.

information can be stored in our short-term memory can naturally vary between different individuals ranging from a matter of a few seconds to a few minutes.

Peterson and Peterson (1959) investigated the duration of working memory and the various factors that cause working memory to decay.[5] They concluded that almost all information stored in short-term memory that is not rehearsed is lost within 18 to 30 seconds! That is alarming when we consider the implications for that in the classroom and this emphasises the importance of repeated exposure to content, concepts, vocabulary and skills. If we do not revisit material it will be lost forever, snatched away by the curse of forgetting (although I will later explain why forgetting isn't always as bad as we may think).

Finally, if information has been rehearsed and retained beyond short-term/working memory then it is then stored in what is known as our long-term memory. But it is not enough to be able to store that information in our long-term memory – we need to be able to retrieve it from there too.

The three stages of memory discussed are classed as the encoding, storage and retrieval stages as shown in figure 2, based on the work of Arthur Melton (1963).[6]

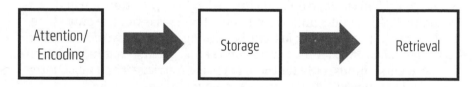

Figure 2 Stages of memory and the learning process

Retrieval storage refers to how well information is embedded in our long-term memory and retrieval strength refers to how easily a piece of information can be brought to mind when required.[7] It is good for teachers to be aware of and consider both retrieval storage and strength.

'Procedural memory' refers to a type of long-term memory that we use on a daily basis, without consciously realising that we do, often known as

---

5. Peterson, L. R. and Peterson, M. J. (1959) 'Short-term retention of individual verbal items', *Journal of Experimental Psychology* 58 pp. 193-198.
6. Melton, A. W. (1963) 'Implications of Short-Term Memory for a General Theory of Memory', *Journal of Verbal Learning and Verbal Behaviour* 2 pp. 1-21
7. Didau, D. and Rose, N. (2016) *What Every Teacher Needs To Know About Psychology*. Woodbridge, Suffolk: John Catt Educational.

autopilot. Automacy involves knowing how to do something so well that we don't stop to consider each stage of the process, it just happens seamlessly and effortlessly. Procedural memory does not require conscious recall, so it is consequently classified as non-declarative memory (declarative memory requires conscious recall and more effort). Procedural memory is important in a school setting because once students are familiar with specific activities or skills, the process becomes automatic so that working memory is freed up and can instead be used to focus on the content or questions instead of how to complete a task.

The retrieval process

I was taking part in a quiz one evening with a group of friends and a question came up that annoyed me. I knew that I did actually know the answer but I just couldn't recall it at that precise moment in time – typical. I'm sure it's a moment that many people can relate to. I started explaining to my friends that the information was there inside my long-term memory but I just couldn't retrieve it. One of my friends rightly asked: 'What good is information and knowledge if it's in your memory but you can't find it or use it?' Exactly. We need to be able to access that information easily when we require it.

As educators our role isn't to simply transfer information to students' long-term memory, we also need to support them so that they can retrieve that information when required. Dr Pooja K. Agarwal – cognitive scientist and co-author of a book I highly recommend, *Powerful Teaching: Unleashing the Science of Learning* – often explains that we shouldn't just focus on getting information into students' mind but instead ask, 'How can we get that information out of their mind?' That is where retrieval practice becomes so crucial to learning.

Paul A. Kirschner, John Sweller and Richard E. Clark are widely quoted for defining learning as a change in long-term memory, 'if nothing has changed nothing has been learned'.[8] This is a very good way of looking at learning, not education as a whole but specifically learning, stressing the importance of long-term memory. This has been the game changer for myself and many other teachers. Long-term memory wasn't part of my vocabulary, understanding or lesson planning when I first began teaching, but it is now.

---

8. Kirschner, P. A., Sweller, J. and Clark, R. E. (2006) 'Why Minimal Guidance During Instruction Does Not Work: An Analysis of the Failure of Constructivist, Discovery, Problem-Based, Experiential, and Inquiry-Based Teaching', *Educational Psychologist* 41 (2) pp. 75-86.

We are constantly retrieving information from memory on a daily basis, sometimes we are aware of it and other times we aren't. When a parent asks their child what did they do or learn in school that day the child has to retrieve the information from memory to answer. Whilst parents who ask their children about their day show genuine parental interest, it can also be a useful retrieval strategy, but are parents aware of this? If so, perhaps they could ask more often or think more carefully about the questions they do ask; perhaps they could even challenge their children by asking them to retrieve what they remember from yesterday, last week and even further back.

Retrieval practice has transformed classrooms around the world with leaders and teachers implementing it into their curriculum planning, lessons and home learning. However, there is still a lot of work to be done in embedding retrieval strategies and ensuring all teachers, students and parents recognise the value of this approach. I know many schools that have fully embraced retrieval practice and it has become part of their language of learning. I am very fortunate to currently work at a school that models exactly this but I am also aware of other schools that haven't recognised retrieval practice at all, or schools where only a select few teachers have done so, isolated in their classroom. Even worse are the schools and leaders who have enforced retrieval practice as simply another tick box activity only to be completed during lesson observations or inspections. How would you describe your school and its approach to retrieval practice? This is something to reflect and consider as a teacher or leader.

The science of learning is another phrase being used in education circles a lot, but it's important that educators, students and parents have a good understanding of what the science of learning actually refers to. Bradley Busch and Edward Watson are authors of the insightful book (described by John Hattie as his 'book of the decade') *The Science of Learning 77 Studies That Every Teacher Needs to Know*, which provides an excellent definition of the science of learning: 'It is the quest to help our students learn more effectively and efficiently.'[9] I couldn't agree more. What could be more important in our role as educators (other than the safety and welfare of our children) to support learning than enlightening ourselves on the science of learning? Learning how to learn has not previously received the profile and importance that it deserves but it certainly has begun to recently.

---

9. Busch, B. and Watson, E. (2019) *The Science of Learning: 77 Studies That Every Teacher Needs to Know.* Abingdon, Oxon: Routledge.

Research

There has been a movement in recent years that has involved more teachers connecting with educational research and becoming more evidence informed. Educational research has never been easier to access, especially with: the Chartered College of Teaching, which provides online access to journals and their magazine *Impact* that members receive; the EduTwitter network online tweeting articles and blogs; and, the increase of events taking place for teachers organised by teachers. There's also a wealth of educational books available too, driven by research written by both teachers and academics. I explore the reasons for the renewed interest in educational research in more depth in the first chapter of this book. However, there are still barriers when it comes to teacher engagement with research. I believe the main obstacles are:

- Time to engage, embed and reflect
- Academic jargon and terminology
- Access to research journals can still prove difficult or costly (although this is improving as mentioned)
- A disconnect between educational research and teachers
- There are inconsistent findings in the field of research linked to education
- Lack of trust and scepticism after neuromyths previously published as educational research are now debunked (learning styles being the classic example)

Probably the most obvious and pressing factor can be time. Teachers are busy. We have planning and marking to do, parents' evenings, pastoral responsibilities, organising school trips and much, much more, in addition to balancing our own personal lives too. How do we find the time to engage with this research?

Many teachers are choosing to do so in their own time because it is interesting, exciting and can be incredibly liberating, but schools do have a responsibility to support teachers who are choosing to become research and evidence informed. It is also something that, as a profession, we should do together. Engaging with educational research is so important; time should be dedicated to this at a whole school, department and individual level. A senior leader at my school recently delivered a presentation about how schools should actively and financially support teachers when it comes to professional learning.

There is research that can seem contradictory at times or not that clear. If it is not consistent then we need to think about how we react and respond to that (although the majority of the research I have encountered in regards to the testing effect is in agreement with similar experiments and findings).

Author of *Why the Brain Matters: A Teacher Explores Neuroscience*, Jon Tibke, points out that 'research is inevitably highly complex, specialised and laden with language unfamiliar to all but those working in the field',[10] and I, at times, have found this to be very true, making for some confusing reading. I have had struggles with educational research, mainly due to the complexity and use of unfamiliar terminology, but ultimately I have persevered and learned a lot despite the challenges.

Experienced teachers can also feel the frustration after witnessing many fads come and go throughout their careers; understandably they are wary of the next short-lived fad being introduced to, once again, later disappear. Another problem linked to educational research is simply the term 'evidence informed' because that in itself poses several questions, such as: where is the evidence from? Is it accurate and reliable? What were the context and conditions of the research carried out? Has the testing or research been replicated?

The Learning Scientists are a team of academic researchers and cognitive psychological scientists that are interested in research on education. Their vision is to make scientific research on learning more accessible to students, teachers and parents. They offer this considered advice in their brilliant book *Understanding How We Learn: A Visual Guide*: 'If evidence supports the effectiveness of a strategy, then we should by all means adopt it, but continue to be flexible as the science evolves.'[11] This is the approach I have taken in regards to educational research – adopting and applying it, but also accepting that we are not there yet. There are many developments yet to be made and much more progress to come, I am sure.

Author Carl Hendrick has reflected that in his view that 'there is an ethical imperative to provide the best possible classroom conditions in which students in our charge can flourish', adding 'this means rejecting what wastes time and embracing that which makes the most use of it',[12]

---

10. Tibke, J. (2019) *Why the Brain Matters: A Teacher Explores Neuroscience*. Thousand Oaks, CA: Corwin.
11. Sumeracki, M., Weinstein, Y. and Caviglioli, O. (2018) *Understanding How We Learn: A Visual Guide*. London: Routledge.
12. Hendrick, C. and Macpherson, R. (2017) *What Does This Look Like In The Classroom? Bridging the Gap Between Research and Practice*. Woodbridge, Suffolk: John Catt Educational.

and I don't think any educator would disagree with that. We have a duty and responsibility to support the students in our care as best we can and we should continually reflect and review as to how we do this. Hendrick recognises research cannot give us all the answers, but it can guide us in the right direction.

Busch and Watson also highlight that 'despite there being a wealth of research on the science of learning, to date, much of it has failed to get into the hands of the people who need it most, e.g. teachers'.[13] I would go further than that and suggest that the people who also need the knowledge and understanding of how we learn are the students themselves. That is why research summaries are so useful because they are more concise, accessible and practical.

Professor John Dunlosky illustrated that there has been too much focus in education on 'what' rather than 'how'. Dunlosky stated: 'Emphasis is on *what* students need to learn, whereas little emphasis – if any – is placed on training students *how* they should go about learning the content and what skills will promote efficient studying to support robust learning. Nevertheless, teaching students *how* to learn is as important as teaching them content, because acquiring both the right learning strategies and background knowledge is important – if not essential – for promoting lifelong learning.'[14]

Learning how to learn has been described by researchers Elizabeth and Robert Bjork as the 'ultimate survival tool',[15] essentially a crucial life skill. I think that description is so powerful and accurate, one that we should share and stress to our students. This is something I have only realised and embraced as an adult, as a student I always focused on the content and subject-specific skills (which no one is suggesting isn't important) rather than consider the learning strategies I was using. I am now very fortunate to be in a position where I can share this information with the learners in my classroom.

I am aware of many schools where senior and middle leaders filter educational research to share with colleagues and provide time during inset days or departmental meetings to get to grips with this research.

13. Busch, B. and Watson, E. (2019) *The Science of Learning: 77 Studies That Every Teacher Needs to Know.* Abingdon, Oxon: Routledge.

14. Dunlosky, J. (2013) 'Strengthening the Student Toolbox: Study Strategies to Boost Learning', *American Educator* 37 (3) pp. 12–21. Retrieved from: www.bit.ly/2iISdYC

15. Bjork, E. and Bjork, R. (2011) 'Making things hard on yourself, but in a good way: Creating desirable difficulties to enhance learning', in Gernsbacher, M. A., Pew, R. W., Hough, L. M., Pomerantz, J. R. (eds) and FABBS Foundation, *Psychology and the real world: Essays illustrating fundamental contributions to.* New York, NY: Worth Publishers, pp. 56–64

Although this is amazing, not all schools are actively doing this. This is something I am presently attempting to incorporate as a middle leader with the teachers in my department. Not all teachers are as enthusiastic to engage with the latest educational research and, as leaders, that can bring many issues and challenges as to how to create a culture of professional learning which is evidence informed whilst not dismissing teacher expertise, experience and autonomy.

I personally prefer research summaries that are concise and clear for teachers to access, understand and act on. I will refer to a wide range of sterling research summaries in this book and recommend further reading after each chapter. This may seem overwhelming, I am certainly not suggesting all of the books are a must-read because – as someone who has read all of the recommended reading – I have noticed a lot of overlap and repetition with content and information, therefore they are simply a selection of recommendations.

In December of 2018 I attended and presented at a wonderful teaching event in Hong Kong, the Asia Pacific International Schools Conference (AISC). One of the main strands and theme of the conference was the science of learning. The keynote speaker for this strand was Dr Jared Cooney Horvath, a former teacher turned author and academic researcher specialising in how we learn. Cooney Horvath is incredibly knowledgeable and passionate about the science of learning but he made it explicitly clear that the experts in the classroom are the teachers, as we have the insight, knowledge and understanding that academic researchers don't (in the same sense they have expertise in their chosen field that teachers do not possess). Cooney Horvath has stated that 'knowing how someone learns and knowing how to guide someone through the process are two very different things'.[16]

In addition to sharing a wide range of sources focusing on educational research I will include anecdotes because, as teachers, we are constantly acquiring a collection of unique experiences and stories that we can reflect on and share with other educators in the same way we can approach educational research. I also reference many blogs written by teachers. There are so many high-quality blogs available to read freely written by successful authors, leaders and teachers which illustrate that, as a profession, the collaborative and reflective culture is thriving.

---

16. The Learning Scientists (2019) 'Episode 40 – Memorizing Facts vs Using Information with Dr. Jared Cooney Horvath', *Learning Scientists* [Podcast] 2 May. Retrieved from: www.bit.ly/2Vp6SJG

I have previously described educational research as one piece of a complex puzzle when it comes to working with children in schools. Retrieval practice is another vital piece of that complex puzzle, however it is only *one* piece of that puzzle. Relationships, routines and much more all make up the other pieces, and what use is a puzzle with a missing piece? All pieces need to be firmly in place and connected. I do want to stress that I – and I am sure that most if not all teachers – believe there is much more to education than retrieval and the ability to recall information. That is undoubtedly an important aspect of the learning process but the bigger picture is much more intricate. I have created an infographic to show some of the different elements (or pieces of the complex puzzle) teachers have to consider when it comes to teaching and learning in the classroom, in addition to retrieval practice. What would you add?

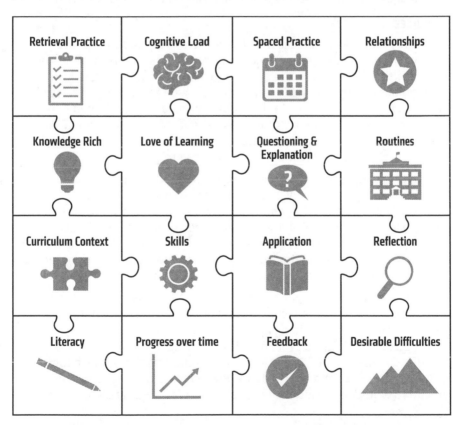

Figure 3 The teaching and learning puzzle

Finally, I have realised how important it is to share this wealth of knowledge, insight and awareness that educational research has provided us with. Other ways I have shared my ideas and reflections have included my blogs, podcast and presenting to colleagues, but sharing this information with my students has had the biggest impact.

In July 2019, I left a school where I had been teaching for three years. I received lots of lovely cards and presents. Something that I was not expecting was the gratitude shown by colleagues, parents and students for introducing them to the science of learning and educational research with a specific focus on retrieval practice. I did introduce retrieval practice to my colleagues and students, at times it came with many obstacles, reluctance and even rejection but it was certainly worth it. The impact was evident with outcomes, results and through the knowledge of knowing others now know more about how we learn.

Resources

All of the resources and ideas in this book are designed to support retrieval practice. The main aspect to remember is that this means no notes, textbooks or support is permitted as it prevents retrieval from taking place (although I will later explore the benefits of *some* retrieval support). Many of the tasks in this book could be easily adapted to be used alongside notes and textbooks as part of the encoding process, which is important but it is not retrieval practice. The key to retrieval practice is the retrieval from memory. It's as simple as that.

Like all things in education, retrieval practice can be carried out and delivered effectively or badly. That is why it is so important that we continually learn and review our practice. When it comes to implementing research and applying this in the classroom we need to think about meaningful learning. What does meaningful teaching and learning look like? This is a very challenging question but also necessary for us to reflect on when planning a sequence of lessons or designing a curriculum.

Karpicke has written about this and I thought he demonstrated that researchers and teachers are not as disconnected as some might assume. Karpicke wrote, in a paper focusing on how retrieval promotes meaningful learning, that meaningful learning is about producing organised, coherent and integrated mental models that allow people to make inferences and apply their knowledge.[17] I am confident all educators would agree with this observation (although teachers may

17. Karpicke, J. (2012) 'Retrieval-Based Learning: Active Retrieval Promotes Meaningful Learning', *Current Directions in Psychological Science* 21 (3) pp. 157-163.

wish to develop this further based on their own interpretations and experiences) and generally that would be widely accepted as an accurate description of meaningful learning. We also need to take this question further by asking what does meaningful learning look like in our subjects/phases that we teach? This was a point I considered when it came to retrieval task design.

I have included many real life examples of resources used in my classroom but as I now only specialise in teaching history I have asked teachers across other subjects, who have used these resources in their subject, to share their examples in this book. Many thanks to the teachers that have kindly agreed to do so. I have also included visuals to once again help you, the reader and teacher, consider how the tasks could be used in your classroom with your learners.

During the early years of my career I spent many evenings printing, cutting, gluing and laminating. I did enjoy creating innovative resources but they were time consuming and added negatively to my workload and wellbeing. On reflection, I also think many of my resources were over complicated and, at times, distracted from learning; knowledge of cognitive load has helped me to consider this aspect too. Now I combine educational research with my professional experience and insight to create resources that are **low effort, high impact**. I believe this to be of paramount importance when creating or using resources in the classroom. The low effort does not refer to students' effort, but rather the time a teacher puts into creating and planning, as they are tasks or activities that are simple and easy to adapt and use.

In my first teaching role I was observed by my deputy headteacher and the feedback he gave me all those years ago has stayed with me and impacted my practice ever since. He observed a religious education lesson where the class were studying key events and ceremonies in different religions at the time. That particular lesson was about Christian weddings and I did a lot of unnecessary preparation. As I wasn't teaching the period before, I used that time to organise and get ready and it took me about 55 minutes just to set up the classroom and resources. I remember decorating the classroom with a wedding theme. There were name cards on each of the desks for students – as would be at a wedding reception for guests – despite the fact students were sitting in their regular seats anyway. I also sprinkled some confetti on tables and hung up white wedding decorations around the room. The extra touches added nothing to the learning (many of the decorations weren't even explicitly linked to Christianity but have evolved as wedding traditions), and only resulted in extra tidying up for me at the end of the lesson. This serves as an example of high effort, low impact.

The feedback my deputy headteacher gave me was very positive (despite the obvious elements of gimmickry and novelty), but he did comment on the amount of effort and attention that had gone into that single lesson and how it would not be possible to do that for every lesson. It was simply unsustainable, unnecessary and unrealistic and he was right; I was very grateful for that constructive feedback.

The high impact refers to impact on learning both inside and outside of the classroom, which is absolutely essential. When teachers aren't spending hours planning and designing classroom activities that frees up our precious time, thus allowing us to develop subject knowledge and professional learning, and even to enjoy our evenings and weekends more – how lovely! I do enjoy lesson planning and being creative with resources, but I finally feel I have struck the balance with **low effort, high impact**.

An excellent resource is not a substitute or replacement for poor subject knowledge, but a resource can certainly compliment subject knowledge to create a meaningful and impactful learning environment. The resources in this book are intended to be combined with teachers' own subject knowledge and adapted for teachers' classrooms.

Retrieval practice can be fun, enjoyable and engaging without gimmickry but with a clear focus on learning. This book contains a wide range of tasks to support retrieval practice with explanations, links to research and classroom context provided. This book is aimed at teachers in the classrooms across primary and secondary, in addition to middle and senior leaders.

All of the resource templates in this book are available to download for free online, with QR codes at the back of this book. Feedback I received after my first book was published, *Love to Teach: Research & Resources for every classroom*, was that the simplicity of the resources and the visual images helped teachers to see how they could implement the ideas and tasks in their classrooms with ease. Subsequently, I have built on this feedback with more templates and downloadable materials available.

There is also a link to a very in-depth and thorough glossary of key terms connected to learning at the back of this book, created and kindly shared by James Mannion. This glossary may include terms that you are familiar with but it is not written in a condescending tone. Since engaging with educational research, my vocabulary has increased considerably as there is a professional dialogue now taking place in schools and online that is continually developing. The glossary created by Mannion goes far beyond retrieval practice and the science of learning, but it is very interesting and great for newly or recently qualified teachers too.

Please feel free to contact me, to provide feedback or ask any questions about retrieval practice. Let me know if, or how, any of my ideas have worked with your classes. You can contact me via my website lovetoteach87.com, send me a tweet @87History or use the hashtag #RetrievalBook.

CHAPTER 1:
WHAT DOES THE
RESEARCH TELL US?

When it comes to educational research on retrieval practice there are a number of questions teachers might ask, for starters: 'Where to begin?', 'Where do I access the research?', 'There's so much research available what should I trust or refer to?' – hopefully, my book will address all of those questions plus more. As a starting point, I have posed some questions that I have considered or know to be raised by other educators in regards to retrieval practice.

Is retrieval practice just about memorising facts?

I think this is a very common misconception about retrieval practice. It is easy to see why retrieval practice could be associated with regurgitating specific facts and rote learning, especially as it is also known as the 'testing effect'. Many schools have also moved towards adopting a knowledge-rich curriculum, so again the assumption can be made that retrieval practice supports the ability to memorise facts (however, knowledge-rich certainly doesn't mean a curriculum built on isolated and cold facts without meaning, understanding, skills or experiences).

Retrieval practice does support the recall of key facts and should be a part of any knowledge-rich curriculum but this strategy has many other benefits for both teachers and learners. Karpicke wrote that, 'practicing retrieval does not merely produce rote, transient learning; it produces meaningful, long-term learning'.[1] We want students to be able to solve problems instead of memorising solutions and be able to make links, connections and provide rich explanations, rather than simply repeat facts, numbers, quotes or dates.

The key piece of research I will use to explain how retrieval practice can offer much more than memorisation is a very useful paper: *Ten*

---

1. Karpicke, J. (2012) 'Retrieval-Based Learning: Active Retrieval Promotes Meaningful Learning', *Current Directions in Psychological Science* 21 (3) pp. 157-163.

Benefits of Testing and Their Applications to Educational Practice by Henry L. Roediger III, Adam L. Putnam and Megan A. Sumeracki. The authors build on the vast amount of experiments and studies that have been conducted and recorded focusing on the testing effect(s). They recognise that the main functions of testing are to evaluate performance and assign grades but this paper explores the various benefits of the testing effect on learning.

The research explicitly defines the difference between the direct and in-direct benefits of retrieval practice. Direct benefits arise from the test itself and indirect benefits refer to the other possible and additional effects that can result from testing. This is quite a thorough and in-depth paper, but below I have summarised the key findings:

1. **Retrieval practice aids later retention**. This is recognised by studies and is probably the most well-known benefit of testing. It is regarded by many as the main benefit and purpose of retrieval practice as it can support academic progress. Cooney Horvath explains this point well when he states that 'every time you retrieve a memory it becomes deeper, stronger and easier to access in the future'.[2] This links back to the Bjork quote that using memory, shapes memory.

2. **Testing identifies gaps in knowledge**. This is an indirect benefit I will regularly refer to in this book because it is very helpful for learners. Retrieval practice can show students what they know (what they are able to recall from memory) and also what they aren't able to recall so this can guide and prioritise their future studies.

3. **Testing causes students to learn more from the next learning episode**. This is referred to as the test potentiation effect. Roediger, Putnam and Sumeracki explain that 'when students take a test then restudy material, they learn more from the presentation than they would if they restudied without taking a test',[3] so studying after a test has been completed will be more productive and effective.

4. **Testing produces better organisation of knowledge**. This is very useful for learners. Testing can help students to connect and structure knowledge, making links and identifying patterns when they have to retrieve information. It is noted that further research into this specific area is required, especially within an educational

2. Cooney Horvath, J. (2019) *Stop Talking, Start Influencing: 12 insights from Brain to Science to Make Your Message Stick*. Chatswood, Australia: Exisle Publishing.

3. Megan Sumeracki may be referred to as Megan Smith (Smith, M.) in some references in accordance with research conducted before she got married.

context, but based on their work, 'the prediction would be that testing improves organisation of knowledge'.

5. **Testing improves transfer of knowledge to new contexts.** It is suggested 'retrieval practice induces readily accessible information that can be flexibly used to solve new problems'. The paper recognises how important this is in regards to lifelong learning, commenting that: 'The purpose of education is to teach students information that they will be able to apply later in school, as well as in life after their schooling has finished.' The idea of retrieval practice being used to support the transfer for knowledge has continued to be studied since and obviously this is of great importance to both teachers and students. Making links between new information and existing knowledge is a central aspect of learning.

6. **Testing can facilitate retrieval of information that was not tested**. I found this factor initially difficult to grasp. When teachers are designing tests or quizzes to use in class, this can be a challenge as there will be restrictions such as timed conditions and the fact that we simply cannot test all the material that has been taught. We have to make careful decisions about what we do decide to ask and how we phrase this too. The research on testing suggests that: 'Retrieval practice does not simply enhance retention of the individual items retrieved during the initial test: taking a test can also produce retrieval-induced facilitation – a phenomenon that shows testing also improves retention of contested but related material.' The authors do recognise that there are contradictory findings published because there is also something referred to as retrieval-induced forgetting (Anderson, Bjork and Bjork 1994), which suggests retrieving some information may actually lead to forgetting other information. This makes sense; if we do not revisit material, we forget it.[4] There have been experiments carried out to differentiate between the conditions impacting both of these factors. The results of the experiments were reviewed and concluded that testing in a classroom can be used to enhance retention of both the material tested and not tested, depending on the conditions.

7. **Testing improves metacognition monitoring**. There is no false sense of confidence with testing (known as the illusion of knowledge), as

---

4. Anderson, M. C., Bjork, R. A. and Bjork, E. L. (1994) 'Remembering can cause forgetting: retrieval dynamics in long-term memory', *Journal of Experimental Psychology* 20 (5) pp. 1063–1087.

the results are very clear and explicit. Metacognition is another term used a lot now but can be difficult to define. It has previously been described as 'thinking about thinking' or 'learning about learning', however it is more complex than that. Metacognition has been ranked by the Education Endowment Foundation (EEF) in their widely-read 'Teaching and Learning Toolkit' as one of the most effective practices for students to support learning. It involves self-monitoring and having an awareness of learning in regards to the behaviours, methods and techniques used. Therefore, this benefit links in with point number two about a student recognising what they know and don't know and what they can do about that. There has been a lot of research and investigation into this field of metacognition. The authors point out that 'students' ability to accurately predict what they know and do not know is an important skill in education, but unfortunately students often make inaccurate predictions'. This is where metacognition is important. Karpicke, in a different research paper, noted that 'retrieval practice is a tool many students lack metacognitive awareness of and do not use as often as they should'.[5] This is true and something I will address later in this chapter.

8. **Testing prevents interference from prior material when learning new material.** There are limitations to the accuracy of this benefit as the research was based mainly on word lists and once again further investigation is required. This refers to the act of using a test to prevent proactive interference, which can occur when content is studied in succession.

9. **Testing provides feedback to instructors.** This point explains how retrieval practice can support and inform teachers in regards to what students know, understand and can recall. This, again, is not something that is new to teachers but, nevertheless, is still very helpful. This demonstrates why we need flexible lesson plans, as we can't always anticipate where the gaps in knowledge or misconceptions will arise but retrieval feedback can give us insight with this.

10. **Frequent testing encourages students to study.** This is, in itself, a brilliant indirect benefit of testing, as a motivational strategy for learners. I have noticed this after embedding retrieval practice as part of my classroom routine, students know this will take place in

5. Karpicke, J. (2012) 'Retrieval-Based Learning: Active Retrieval Promotes Meaningful Learning', *Current Directions in Psychological Science* 21 (3) pp. 157-163.

my lessons and they can plan for this. I can recall occasions where students have been successful in a retrieval task in the lesson and told me that they had been practising retrieval at home to prepare for upcoming quizzes. This fills me with so much joy, happiness and pride as a teacher. Watching students develop and take ownership and responsibility for their learning really is very special indeed.

I have created an infographic summary of the ten benefits of the testing effect based on this study. This could be a helpful overview for sharing with colleagues, students and parents. We shouldn't think of retrieval practice as simply recalling detached or random facts and the benefits illustrate this.

1 Supports later retention and retrieval

2 Identifies gaps in knowledge

3 Testing causes students to learn more from the next study episode

4 Better organisation of knowledge

5 Improves transfer of knowledge to new contexts

6 Facilitates retrieval of material that was not tested

7 Improves metacognition

8 Prevents interference form previous material when learning new content

9 Provides valuable feedback to teachers

10 Regular testing encourages students to study more

Figure 1 The ten benefits of the testing effect

Further benefits include how retrieval practice can be used to close the vocabulary gap and support vocabulary instruction in the classroom. Retrieval tasks can be used with terminology, definitions and using vocabulary in different contexts. I also think it is a relatively easy strategy to implement and embed, although it can come with some challenges and workload issues, it is certainly possible to make retrieval practice part of a regular classroom routine.

Another obvious yet understated benefit of retrieval practice is how satisfying it is to answer a question correctly or recall information without support or having to search for it online. Why else do so many people enjoy going to quiz events or watching quiz shows on TV? I know a lot of people who take great pleasure when they are able to answer a challenging question whilst watching *University Challenge* and my students have often expressed delight after a successful result in a test or quiz. However, to do this requires retrieval success. Failure to answer correctly can lead to retrieval frustration but learning isn't easy, therefore failure is an undeniable aspect of the learning process too.

How long should we wait before testing students on previously covered material?

Forgetting has often been viewed negatively, and understandably so after a teacher has invested so much time, effort and dedication teaching content to their students only for them to forget (through no fault of their own)! We are all guilty of forgetting, it happens. It can be frustrating when students forget things that we felt, as teachers, we explained well and clearly. We must prepare for forgetting and accept this as part of the learning process.

A teacher looking to implement retrieval practice into their long- and short-term planning will want to know how much time to leave between study sessions to best support learning and recall. It is recognised and accepted that retrieval practice will be more effective if teachers allow for some forgetting to take place before we ask students to try to retrieve that information. The forgetting increases the challenge and the level of challenge increases the effectiveness.

Should this space of time between the encoding and retrieval stages be a matter of days, weeks, or even months? It would be really helpful for teachers to know the optimal amount of time to leave before testing students on previously-covered material, to further support planning and to instruct students with their own spaced practice.

Unfortunately, this is a question that we do not have an exact answer for but there are recommendations that act as a very helpful guide. This question is continually being explored and looked into by researchers. There was a study conducted in 2008 that focused on optimal spacing. The research paper covering this study is 'Spacing Effects in Learning A Temporal Ridgeline of Optimal Retention',[6] which I found to be quite a complex and complicated read. The authors stated that: 'The goal of the present study was to examine the joint effects of gap and RI (retention intervals) more systematically and over longer time intervals than has been done previously.'

This wasn't the first study to look into this question and this study required running thousands of training sessions and tests in a laboratory setting. This study involved 1354 students that were all set the task to learn 32 trivia facts. Already we can see that this experiment was not carried out in classroom conditions and the students were given a task to recall random facts that we do not typically teach in schools; facts are generally connected to a bigger picture and topic, as part of a cohesive curriculum. Nevertheless, the results can still prove to be informative.

Students' answers were compared and analysed to find out what the optimum amount of time to leave between study sessions should be. As expected, the results demonstrated that spacing was more effective than cramming and the further away the test is the longer the gaps should be. The authors observed that: 'Working memory operates on a time scale of seconds or minutes, whereas gap effects are seen on a scale of days and weeks (the optimal gap was several weeks for our longer retention intervals).' They also added that 'to achieve enduring retention, people must usually study information on multiple occasions'.

This does reiterate the point about waiting days and weeks for retention intervals. Another factor that will determine the optimum interval between study sessions is how far in the future a test is being taken. So if it is one week, the suggested spacing should be one to two days; one month until the test would result in a one-week interval; two months would be two weeks; six months would be three weeks; and, up to a year could include a four-week interval between sessions. As teachers we can also use our professional judgment in addition to the knowledge and understanding that we should allow for some time to elapse to allow forgetting before retrieval practice takes place, after all it is a strategy to retrieve information from long-term memory, not short-term memory.

6. Cepeda, N. J., Vul, E., Rohrer, D., Wixted, J. T. and Pashler, H. (2008) 'Spacing Effects in Learning: A Temporal Ridgeline of Optimal Retention', *Psychological Science* 19 (11) pp. 1095-1102.

Bush and Watson suggest 'as a rule of thumb, the closer you are to forgetting a piece of information (before it completely drops out of the brain), the more likely it is that you will benefit from revisiting it.'[7] On reflection, I know that I have revisited content too soon and not delved further back, or perhaps even waited far too long before revisiting material again, thus meaning that the content required relearning. Many of the tasks in this book support striking the balance when it comes to forgetting and retrieval. Research has shown than any spaced practice is better than no spacing,[8] so we shouldn't become too concerned within specific time delays.

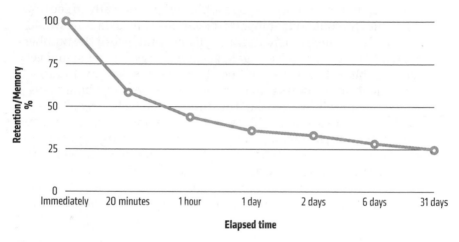

Figure 2 Ebbinghaus' forgetting curve (1885)

The forgetting curve shown in figure 2 is based on the work of German researcher and psychologist Hermann Ebbinghaus and the results from the study mentioned above also emphasise the accuracy of this gradual process of forgetting. This model is now quite well known amongst teachers and certainly respected amongst academic researchers interested in the fields of retrieval and spaced practice. This information only became mainstream in recent years, despite the fact that the findings of this experiment were published in 1885. There have been some critics (within the educational field) of the forgetting curve, mainly focusing on the point that the research is from the 19th century and consequently must be outdated and incorrect, but this simply isn't true.

7. Busch, B. and Watson, E. (2019) *The Science of Learning: 77 Studies That Every Teacher Needs to Know.* Abingdon, Oxon: Routledge.
8. Carpenter, S. K. and Agarwal, P. K. (2019) *How to use spaced retrieval practice to boost learning.* Ames, IA: Iowa State University.

Another reason why some people have been sceptical or dubious about the forgetting curve is due to the unusual fact that Ebbinghaus conducted the experiment on himself, to test his own memory and the length of time it would take for new information to be forgotten. This is clearly not how research is carried out today. Ebbinghaus memorised lists of what he called 'nonsense syllables' that had no semantic associations (deep meaning), which is obviously different to what we do in schools as we focus on retrieving content with significance that can be applied in different contexts.

Ebbinghaus would write down the nonsense syllables in the correct order with accuracy and then continue to test himself periodically to see how many syllables he could remember. After various time delays he would attempt to relearn the list of nonsense syllables and record the numbers of rehearsals he would require to gain accuracy. This doesn't sound very sophisticated but Ebbinghaus was one of the first researchers to carry out experiments and studies into how the memory works. Ebbinghaus discovered that his ability to recall the information he had memorised quickly declined, subsequently his work still remains influential today. The forgetting curve by Ebbinghaus shows how forgetting happens after the initial period of learning has taken place, occurring rapidly in the first instance then slowing down. It illustrates that once information has been encoded, then the first 20 minutes after this are prone to forgetting. Within roughly an hour the majority of that new information will be forgotten. The curve shows that after the first day, forgetting occurs at a slower pace.

Despite the conditions of this original experiment it has since been replicated many times by different researchers and cognitive psychologists. The repeated studies demonstrated similar results. One experiment carried out had a subject spend 70 hours learning lists and relearning them after 20 minutes, after an hour, nine hours, a day or 31 days. The results were similar to the original conclusion Ebbinghaus came to.[9] He suggested that all individuals forget new information in a similar manner and at a similar rate, regardless of the content and complexity. Studies have also shown that using spaced practice instead of cramming for a range of tasks, including recalling keywords, facts or complex maths problems, can result in a 10-30% difference in the final test outcomes.[10]

9. Murre, J. M. J. and Dros, J. (2015) 'Replication and Analysis of Ebbinghaus' forgetting curve', PLoS One 10 (7). Retrieved from: www.bit.ly/2zNeTgY
10. Busch, B. and Watson, E. (2019) The Science of Learning: 77 Studies That Every Teacher Needs to Know. Abingdon, Oxon: Routledge.

When we check understanding during or at the end of a lesson, the information will likely still be in a student's short-term memory. If we wait too long to check if knowledge has been retained then that information can be forgotten and will then need to be relearned again. However, if we wait for some forgetting to occur and then use retrieval practice, the strategy will strengthen the information to counteract the forgetting curve. Author and educational myth buster Pedro De Bruyckere has written about this at length, he emphasises that forgetting is crucial for learning, which sounds like an oxymoron but does show that forgetting is an important stage in the learning process.

Consequently, the forgetting curve has very powerful implications for memory and learning. Careful planning and factoring in retrieval and spaced practice into lessons can interrupt the forgetting process and support long-term memory.

Where does retrieval practice fit into a lesson, scheme of work or curriculum?

To address this question I will focus on the renowned and celebrated research and work of Barak Rosenshine and Tom Sherrington.

Barak Rosenshine's Principles of Instruction has become a popular research summary that teachers and leaders around the world are referring to and it is often used to guide curriculum and lesson planning. I think it has become so popular and widely used because it is free to access; it is summarised without any academic jargon and quite short, thus making it accessible, coherent and less time consuming to read. It is a comprehensive paper (perfect for teachers looking to engage with research) that incorporates practical implications for the classroom. The principles have a common sense approach that teachers find themselves nodding along to in agreement. Sherrington has stated that he was 'struck immediately by its brilliant clarity, simplicity and its potential to support teachers seeking to engage with cognitive science and the wider world of education research',[11] again emphasising why it has been so well received by teachers.

Rosenshine's Principles of Instruction stem from three different sources and I believe these different sources produce a winning combination. Firstly, research in cognitive science and how the brain encodes and stores information. Secondly, research on cognitive support with strategies to help students learn complex material. Finally, evidence

---

11. Sherrington, T. (2019) *Rosenshine's Principles in Action*. Woodbridge, Suffolk: John Catt Educational.

based on the work of 'master teachers'. The master teachers, as described by Rosenshine, are 'those teachers whose classrooms made the highest gains on achievement tests'. Fusing together these different strands of research and experience, Rosenshine has devised a set of principles that are universal in education.

Below is a brief summary of the ten key principles that are outlined by Rosenshine with an explanation as to how it can link with retrieval practice in the classroom:

1. **Start the lesson with a short review of previous learning.** This can be achieved through various tasks, which is essentially what this book consists of – retrieval practice. Sherrington adds that: 'Students don't necessarily recall recent learning readily and it pays to anticipate this rather than be frustrated by this.'[12] This was transformative for my own morale as a teacher because I would often feel at a loss when it seemed students understood a concept, event or information, then at a later date that notion or memory had vanished, much to my disappointment. Now I can be ready for this with my planning. To reiterate, we need to accept it is part of the learning process and not a reflection on us as a teacher. It is important to add that retrieval practice does not have to be restricted to the start of a lesson but can in fact be used at any point within a lesson. Continual retrieval in a lesson, through tasks, discussions and questioning will be more effective than isolated tasks that simply recall facts, allowing for links and connections to be further developed. I have found the best way to start my lessons is to ensure that retrieval becomes routine.

2. **Present new material and information to students in small and manageable steps.** Ensure student practice after each step, before moving onto new material. This is not the retrieval stage because it's important to remember we can't ask students to retrieve information that isn't actually in their long-term memory, it needs to get there first.

3. **Ask a large number of questions,** checking the response from all the learners in the classroom. A common mistake is to accept answers from some members of the class, and then assume everyone else has that same level of understanding, which is why we need to ensure every learner in the class has the opportunity to retrieve information from memory – not just a few students that have been selected by the teacher.

---

12. Ibid.

4. **Provide students with models and worked examples to support problem solving.** A worked example is where a problem has been shown to the class, with every part of the process explicitly explained through a teacher demonstration, and the problem has been correctly solved. The students will then apply this process or concept to another problem or question. This strategy is best used with novice learners, as it is not regarded as an effective strategy to use with expert learners.[13] Again, this is not a strategy used at the retrieval stage.

5. **Continue to guide student practice.** Rosenshine stated that research findings tell us that 'it is not enough simply to present students with new material, because the material will be forgotten unless there is sufficient rehearsal'.[14] This can be achieved through questioning, additional explanations, consolidation tasks and students summarising the main points of the lesson content. Graham Nuthall suggested in his brilliant book *The Hidden Lives of Learners* (where he and his team spent a significant amount of time in classrooms working with students and teaching, then writing up their findings and reflections) that students need to encounter information at least three times before they understand a concept and that they need opportunities to approach new material in different ways.[15] The power of three in the classroom is very important. After the information has been encountered and encoded then we can later focus on retrieval.

6. **Continually check student understanding,** addressing any misconceptions and supporting the process needed to move new information to long-term memory in order to retrieve at a later date. Busch and Watson also explain that 'just because something has been taught, does not mean it has been deeply learned. Topics must be revisited and retaught. Only by doing this can we help students overcome the forgetting curve and maximise their learning.'[16]

7. **Ensure students obtain a high success rate in the lesson.** A success rate of 80% shows that students are learning the material, and it also shows that the students are challenged[17] (the Goldilocks principle – getting the level of challenge just right!). The same principle can be

---

13. Hirsch, E. D. (2016) *Why Knowledge Matters: Rescuing Our Children from Failed Educational Theories.* Cambridge, MA: Harvard Education Press.
14. Rosenshine, B. (2012) 'Principles of Instruction: Research-Based Strategies That All Teachers Should Know', *American Educator* 36 (1) pp. 12–19. Retrieved from: www.bit.ly/1TczlvF
15. Nuthall, G. (2007) *The Hidden Lives of Learners.* Wellington, New Zealand: NZCER Press.
16. Busch, B. and Watson, E. (2019) *The Science of Learning: 77 Studies That Every Teacher Needs to Know.* Abingdon, Oxon: Routledge.
17. Ibid. (n 14)

applied with retrieval practice, getting the balance right between retrieval difficulty and retrieval success.

8. **Provide scaffolding for students with difficult tasks, ensuring depth and challenge for all**. Rosenshine states, 'a scaffold is a temporary support that is used to assist a learner',[18] and will eventually be removed as the student progresses. Once the scaffolding has been removed then we are requiring students to remember information without any form of support.

9. **Require, monitor and promote independent practice in the classroom**. Rosenshine explains that 'in a typical teacher-led classroom, guided practice is followed by independent practice – by students working alone and practicing the new material. This independent practice is necessary because a good deal of practice (overlearning) is needed in order to become fluent and automatic in a skill.'[19] Again, this focuses on the relevance of automacy in the classroom.

10. **Engage students in regular review**, this can be weekly and/or monthly to revisit prior learning and support long-term memory. Once again this is the area of Rosenshine's Principles of Instruction that lends itself perfectly to retrieval and spaced practice.

Sherrington has explored Rosenshine's principles in great depth. Sherrington regularly delivers presentations around the world, has written many blogs and has also authored the very successful and practical book *Rosenshine's Principles in Action*. I think it would be fair to say this has likely been the most widely-read educational book of 2019 with schools ordering copies in bulk. Sherrington describes Rosenshine's Principles of Instruction as being 'rooted in evidence that has stood the test of time'.[20] I hope these principles now become an integral part of teacher training and on-going professional dialogue and reflection.

Retrieval practice is a central element of Rosenshine's Principles of Instruction. Sherrington has also delved deeper into retrieval practice, which I have explored and created an infographic on this in figure 3 to summarise his points because I think his advice is marvellous and should be considered as the core principles when referring to retrieval practice in the classroom.

18. Rosenshine, B. (2012) 'Principles of Instruction: Research-Based Strategies That All Teachers Should Know', *American Educator* 36 (1) pp. 12-19. Retrieved from: www.bit.ly/1TczlvF
19. Ibid.
20. Sherrington, T. (2019) *Rosenshine's Principles in Action*. Woodbridge, Suffolk: John Catt Educational.

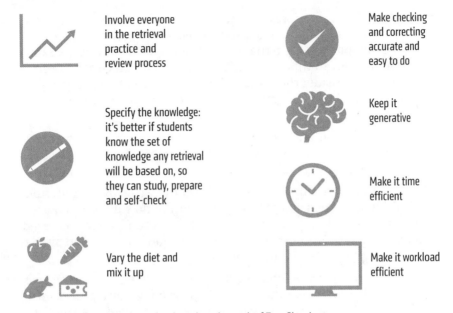

Figure 3 Retrieval practice principles, based on the work of Tom Sherrington

Involve everyone. Sherrington says: 'Good techniques involve all students checking their knowledge, not just a few and not just one at a time as you might do when questioning.'

This is a message I have been sharing with colleagues based on my own experiences and reflections. At the start of a lesson I would often ask a question about the content covered last lesson and usually accept the answer from one selected student but then quickly move on, assuming the rest of the class had this same level of recall or understanding. In hindsight I now know this was not good practice. If, for example, Ben answered my question and provided an explanation about previously-covered material then he has shown he can retrieve that information. However, Ben did all the work and retrieval effort for everyone in the class. No one else had to the opportunity to retrieve that information so that was a missed learning opportunity. All of the retrieval tasks in this book focus on 'retrieval for every student' in the classroom.

Make checking accurate and easy. Sherrington says: 'It should be possible for all students to find out what they got right and wrong, what they know well and where they have gaps.'

This links with the indirect benefits of retrieval practice. Dylan Wiliam has stated that 'the best person to mark a test is the person who has just took it'.[21] Therefore, if we can create and design retrieval activities that enable students to self-check and correct their answers in an accurate yet simple way, then that is ideal. Many of the online quizzing tools recommended in this book will check, mark and record answers with ease. Also, consider the workload implications of this reducing unnecessary and time-consuming marking for the busy teacher (that being every teacher).

Specify the knowledge. Sherrington says: *'Where appropriate, it's better if students know the set of knowledge any retrieval will be based on, so they can study, prepare and self-check.'*

I think this is another important and valid point raised by Sherrington and it links in with retrieval practice being low or no stakes to reduce the anxiety associated with testing. Retrieval success can lead to increased confidence and satisfaction, we do not want to add pressure and pitch the level of challenge too high (not too low either).

Keep it generative. Sherrington says: *'Students need to explore their memory to check what they know and understand. This means removing cue-cards, prompts, scaffolds and cheat sheets; it means closing the books and making students think for themselves.'*

Removing notes, supports and prompts that will prevent students from retrieving information from memory is key. This is more challenging but ultimately more effective for learning and recall. There are resources in the next chapter that remove any form of support or cue to strengthen retrieval. Agarwal states in her very handy *Retrieval Practice Guide:* 'Retrieval practice makes learning effortful and challenging. Because retrieving information requires mental effort, we often think we are doing poorly if we can't remember something. We may feel like progress is slow, but that's when our best learning takes place. The more difficult the retrieval practice, the better it is for long-term learning'.[22]

Vary the diet. Mix it up. Sherrington says: *'This will allow students to explore their schemata in different ways, strengthening future recall.'*

Variety (not in the sense of different learning styles) with task design and creation is imperative and I am really pleased that Sherrington has addressed this point because without the variety there is potential for drill overkill. There is the option to set the same style quiz/test every

21. Hendrick, C. and Macpherson, R. (2017) *What Does This Look Like In The Classroom? Bridging the Gap Between Research and Practice.* Woodbridge, Suffolk: John Catt Educational.
22. Agarwal, P. K., Roediger, H. L., McDaniel, M. A. and McDermott, K. N. (2018) *How to use retrieval practice to improve learning.* Retrieved from: www.bit.ly/2dR3t3R

lesson and whilst I do believe activities and resources should be repeated (especially if the resources are effective and **low effort, high impact**) this can become boring and mundane. The aim of this book in regards to resources was to share a wide variety of stimulating tasks to carry out retrieval practice through different types of quizzing and activities. I think this is another benefit of retrieval practice – it is a flexible strategy that can be adapted in so many ways, for example with or without technology, using pens, paper, mini whiteboards or no equipment at all. There are many possibilities that are explored in the following chapters that aim to mix it up with retrieval practice as Sherrington has suggested. Building on this further, Bjork and Bjork have also discussed varying the conditions in the classroom. They write 'varying the learning context, types of task or practice, rather than keeping them constant or predictable improves later retention, even though it makes learning harder in the short term'.[23] Variety is something we tend to be very good at and strive for in our lessons.

Make it time efficient. Sherrington says: 'A good technique can be used repeatedly in an efficient manner without dominating whole lessons.'

This is also essential because we do have a lot of content that needs to be delivered and consolidated, so retrieval practice needs to be embedded without dominating lesson time or causing disruption to a planned curriculum. Many of the retrieval tasks in this book can be completed within the eight to ten minutes suggested by Rosenshine himself.

Make it workload efficient. Sherrington says: 'The best methods do not involve the teacher checking the students' answer, creating unsustainable workload.'

This links in with the second point about making checking accurate and easy. Technology can also be used to support retrieval practice in addition to reducing teacher workload. Workload is very important and if retrieval practice activities are significantly contributing to a teacher's workload then it will be unrealistic or unsustainable for retrieval practice to become embedded as part of a classroom routine.

It is important to add that Sherrington has warned that Rosenshine's principles should not be turned into a checklist; it should be used as a guide for professional learning,[24] which can become an issue when a concept, idea or trend becomes so popular and embraced by schools.

---

23. Bjork, E. and Bjork, R. (2011) 'Making things hard on yourself, but in a good way: Creating desirable difficulties to enhance learning', in Gernsbacher, M. A., Pew, R. W., Hough, L. M. and Pomerantz, J. R. (eds) & FABBS Foundation, *Psychology and the real world: Essays illustrating fundamental contributions to society.* New York, NY, US: Worth Publishers, pp. 56–64.
24. Sherrington, T. (2018) 'Exploring Barak Rosenshine's seminal Principles of Instruction: Why it is THE must-read for all teachers', *Teacherhead* [Online] 10 June. Retrieved from: www.bit.ly/2MqX54r

Sherrington does also make it very clear that teachers don't need to be concerned about applying every principle, every lesson – that would clearly be unrealistic. He writes, 'different lessons in a learning sequence will require a different focus'.[25] These principles have generated excitement and enthusiasm amongst teachers but we can learn from previous lessons taught to us as a profession not to get too carried away.

In regards to curriculum, which has become another focal point in education recently, teachers and leaders need to be exploring and discussing what to include and not to include in their curriculum and consider why they have chosen to do so. As a middle leader and teacher I noticed that by introducing and embedding more retrieval practice into lessons this could potentially result in less lesson content being covered. At primary and Key Stage 3 this is possible with a more flexible curriculum, but at Key Stages 4 and 5 it is essential that all content is covered, so this can prove to be problematic.

At Key Stage 3 my colleagues and I made the decision to take a 'less is more approach' instead of rushing through content, but rather providing breadth, depth and lots of opportunities for retrieval practice. Mary Myatt has authored many superb books and her latest book *The Curriculum: Gallimaufry to coherence*, is completely dedicated to the topic of curriculum with curriculum planning and review. I would highly recommend this book for middle and senior leaders. Myatt states 'it is never going to be possible to do it all. And we need to live with that'.[26] Absolutely. Retrieval practice is likely to lead to curriculum and lesson planning adjustments but in the long term it will be worth it.

Retrieval practice and other strategies need to be considered and introduced into the curriculum, not as a standalone task in a lesson – which I did initially do before further reading and reflection – but as part of a clear and coherent curriculum with evident progress over time. When reading about the resources in this book you can reflect and ask where in your curriculum would this task support and enhance teaching and learning, thus planning for learning not a lesson.

25. Sherrington, T. (2019) 'Rosenshine's Principles: 10 FAQs', *Teacherhead* [Online] 2 October. Retrieved from: www.bit.ly/2oRA9Rf
26. Myatt, M. (2018) *The Curriculum: Gallimaufry to coherence*. Woodbridge, Suffolk: John Catt Educational.

Is retrieval practice more effective than other revision strategies, and if so why?

The answer to this is simply 'yes'. This is a question that students and parents have asked me many times. I am always happy to explain and articulate why retrieval practice is so powerful and effective, especially in comparison to other more commonly used revision techniques. I have delivered assemblies and presentations focusing on this exact question because it is raised so often, demonstrating a reluctance to accept and embrace retrieval practice. The authors of the ultimate book in the science of learning category, *Make It Stick: The Science of Successful Learning,* write that if you're good at learning you have an advantage in life[27] and we desperately want all of our students to have that advantage.

There is a lot of research available that suggests highlighting and re-reading (amongst some other commonly-used techniques, such as underlining) are not as effective when it comes to revision in comparison to retrieval practice. An excellent research summary to explain why some revision techniques are better than others is *Strengthening The Student Toolbox Study Strategies to Boost Learning* by Professor John Dunlosky.

Dunlosky is regarded as an expert and widely respected in the field of educational research and effective study strategies. Dunlosky and his colleagues reviewed the effectiveness of ten of the most commonly used and popular revision techniques. These strategies were:

1. Retrieval practice with **self-testing** includes taking tests or practice tests on to-be-learned material.

2. **Distributed practice** is also known as spaced practice. Implementing a schedule of practice that spreads out study activities over time instead of forced together.

3. **Interleaved practice** is implementing a schedule of practice that mixes different kinds of problems, or a schedule of study that mixes different kinds of material and topics within a single study session.

4. **Elaboration** is generating an explanation for why an explicitly stated fact or concept is true.

5. **Self-explanation** is explaining how new information is related to known information, or explaining steps taken during problem solving.

---

27. Brown, P. C., Roediger, H. L. and McDaniel, M. A. (2014) *Make It Stick: The Science of Successful Learning.* Cambridge, MA: Harvard Education Press.

6. **Re-reading** includes re-studying text material again after an initial reading, repeated exposure and repeated reading.

7. **Highlighting and underlining** by marking potentially important portions of to-be-learned materials while reading.

8. **Summarisation** looks at writing summaries of to-be-learned texts.

9. **Keyword mnemonics** includes using keywords and mental imagery to associate verbal materials.

10. **Imagery for text** looks at attempting to form mental images of text materials while reading or listening.

Dunlosky stated that his findings revealed 'all of the strategies we reviewed can be used successfully by a motivated student who (at most) has access to a pen or pencil, some index cards, and perhaps a calendar'. This is clearly good news and any revision is better than no revision, which – despite being obvious – we should emphasise to our students. However, despite the research, a motivated student can learn and retain information from any of the ten tested techniques, some were deemed more effective than others. He added, 'we rated two strategies – practice testing and distributed practice – as the most effective of those we reviewed because they can help students regardless of age, they can enhance learning and comprehension of a large range of materials, and, most important, they can boost student achievement'.[28] This is the research for me that has transformed how I view revision strategies and I continually pass on and share these findings. The research summary itself is explained in a clear and accessible format, thus making it a great resource to share with colleagues, students and parents which I highly recommend doing.

Retrieval practice has frequently been compared to highlighting, with many of my students preferring highlighting to retrieval practice. This point links with several experiments I have read about that were carried out to find out whether students prefer to re-study or test themselves. Research carried out by Kornell and Bjork (2007), Karpicke in (2009) and Vaughn and Kornell (2019) were all consistent with their findings that students prefer the option to re-study over self-testing.

Karpicke, Butler and Roediger surveyed 177 college students in 2009 about their study choices and preferences.[29] The study asked students to

28. Dunlosky, J. (2013) 'Strengthening the Student Toolbox: Study Strategies to Boost Learning', *American Educator* 37 (3) pp. 12-21. Retrieved from: www.bit.ly/2iISdYC

29. Karpicke, J. D., Butler, A. C. and Roediger, H. L. (2009) 'Metacognitive strategies in student learning: Do students practise retrieval when they study on their own?', *Memory* 17 (4) pp. 471-479.

list strategies they used when studying and to select whether they would re-read or rehearse recall after studying a textbook chapter. The options to the second question posed were:

1. Go back and re-study either all of the material or parts of it.

2. Try to recall the material without re-studying afterward.

3. Do something else.

57% of students responded that they would re-study/re-read their notes or textbook, 21% answered that they would do something else and only 18% said they would attempt to test themselves and recall material.

The abstract to this paper summarised: 'The results of both questions point to the same conclusion: A majority of students repeatedly read their notes or textbook (despite the limited benefits of this strategy), but relatively few engage in self-testing or retrieval practice while studying. We propose that many students experience illusions of competence while studying and that these illusions have significant consequences for the strategies students select when they monitor and regulate their own learning.'[30]

This probably won't surprise teachers – it is likely most teachers have had similar experiences with their classes (I certainly have) especially teachers of older students/exam classes. This is not to be dismissive of the research, as I have mentioned it can, at times, confirm our instincts, deepen our understanding, and support our experiences as educators.

A considerable amount of my students like highlighting their written work. Highlighting and underling often makes their notes look beautiful, colourful and organised. Parents have also told me they like highlighting as a revision strategy for their children because it shows visible learning has taken place but then I ask does it really show that learning has taken place? Notes that are highlighted do not equate to material that has been learned or can be retrieved from long-term memory.

Why do students prefer re-study over testing? It seems obvious why highlighting is a popular revision strategy, it is more enjoyable than retrieval practice because there is one singular difference between the two strategies – challenge. There is no challenge or very little mental effort required when highlighting notes in comparison to trying to retrieve information when answering questions. The same

30. Karpicke, J. D., Butler, A. C. and Roediger, H. L. (2009) 'Metacognitive strategies in student learning: Do students practise retrieval when they study on their own?', *Memory* 17 (4) pp. 471-479.

can be said for cramming versus spaced practice. Spacing learning over time requires careful planning and organisation (from teachers and students) and it doesn't feel as easy, familiar or comfortable as crammed practice does. It is the challenge from retrieval and spaced practice that significantly improves learning.[31] Brown *et al* wrote that when learning is harder, it's stronger and lasts longer,[32] they also add that the more effort required to retrieve something, the better you actually learn it.[33]

A recent study was carried out by Vaughn and Kornell (2019) with the aim of trying to make learners choose to self-test more often, over re-study, as a strategy.[34] Many experiments have illustrated that retrieval is more effective than re-study and many studies have shown that students prefer re-study over retrieval, but this was designed to find out how to make testing part of a self-motivated study routine that participants actually wanted to do – making testing desirable.

Initially, Vaughn and Kornell made the hypothesis that 'people like to be tested as long as they have a good chance of getting the answer right', linking back to my point about the level of challenge and effort involved having an impact on the study choices students make. Vaughn and Kornell further added that they believed, 'when a person does not have good knowledge of the information they prefer re-study, but when they reach a certain level of competence they prefer to be tested.' They then put this hypothesis to the test in the research they conducted and tried to find out how to make learners choose to test themselves more often because retrieval has to actually be used in order for it to actually be an effective study.

After undertaking differing experiments, they concluded that 'in summary, hints catalysed people's intuitive desire to self-test, without any downside for learning, thus making their self-regulated study more enjoyable and effective.' Providing some aspect of support with hints and providing a possibility of retrieval success meant participants were more willing to use self-testing over re-studying.

Cooney Horvath has also written about the effectiveness of highlighting in comparison to retrieval practice. He wrote that: 'Highlighting text is a great technique to help guide your eyes, focus your attention on

31. Carpenter, S. K. and Agarwal, P. K. (2019) *How to use spaced retrieval practice to boost learning*. Ames, IA: Iowa State University.
32. Brown, P. C., Roediger, H. L. and McDaniel, M. A. (2014) *Make It Stick: The Science of Successful Learning*. Cambridge, MA: Harvard Education Press, p. 9
33. Ibid., p. 82.
34. Vaughn, K. E. and Kornell, N. (2019) 'How to activate students' natural desire to test themselves', *Cognitive Research: Principles and Implications* 4 (4). Retrieved from: www.bit.ly/2BhWMkn

key topics and locate key ideas. Unfortunately, highlighting won't deepen your memory.'[35] This is interesting because it is not completely dismissive of highlighting as it can be a great starting point for revision as long as a student goes back to the highlighted notes and actually does *something* with the highlighted information, for example create a quiz based on the facts, ideas or terms highlighted. We need to have this conversation with our students: 'You have highlighted your notes, now what? How can you ensure that highlighted information is transferred and retrieved from your long-term memory?'

Busch and Watson, building on the work of Dunlosky and others, stress that 'each minute spent highlighting or re-reading is 60 seconds not spent doing something more effective'.[36] Time is precious and learning time is *very* precious, both inside and outside of the classroom. We need to ensure that students are organised with their time and preparation in addition to being informed in regards to the tasks and strategies they use.

The Learning Scientists have also discussed this issue at length and have made the observation that 'students re-reading provides a false sense of confidence in comparison to practice testing'.[37] They add that 're-reading feels good. The more we read a passage, the more fluently we are able to read it. However, reading fluency does not mean we're engaging with information on a deep level, let alone learning it such that we can actually remember it and use it in the future.'[38] This sense of familiarity and fluency then leads to the deceptive illusion of knowing.

The strategies that students find the most enjoyable and satisfying are often those deemed as the least effective. Re-reading does make the reader feel more familiar with the content as they have had repeated exposure to it, but the only way to check that the material has actually been learned and is retrievable is through testing and quizzing. Students are generally poor at judging what they know and understand[39] but testing can support them with this. Retrieval practice and distributed (spaced) practice were recorded as the two most effective study techniques and in Chapter 3 there are examples of how these two strategies can be combined together, both inside and outside of the classroom.

35. Cooney Horvath, J. (2019) *Stop Talking, Start Influencing: 12 insights from Brain to Science to Make Your Message Stick*. Chatswood, Australia: Exisle Publishing, pp. 190–191.
36. Busch, B. and Watson, E. (2019) *The Science of Learning: 77 Studies That Every Teacher Needs to Know*. Abingdon, Oxon: Routledge, p. 5.
37. Sumeracki, M., Weinstein, Y. and Caviglioli, O. (2018) *Understanding How We Learn: A Visual Guide*. Abingdon, Oxon: Routledge, p. 4.
38. Ibid., p. 24.
39. Smith, M. and Firth, J. (2018) *Psychology in the Classroom: A Teacher's Guide To What Works*. Abingdon, Oxon: Routledge, p. 60.

Does retrieval practice lead to more exam pressure, anxiety and stress?

This is a concern that has been raised by colleagues and parents as the wellbeing of students is paramount, and rightly so. I would not be advocating the use of retrieval practice if it were reported to have a negative impact on mental health and wellbeing. However, the opposite has been suggested. Retrieval practice can reduce stress and increase confidence both in the classroom and when students undertake exams.

A key research paper that focused on this exact topic was 'Classroom-based programs of retrieval practice reduce middle school and high school students' test anxiety' by Pooja K. Agarwal, Laura D'Antonio, Henry L. Roediger III, Kathleen B. McDermott and Mark A. McDaniel, which first appeared in the *Journal of Applied Research in Memory and Cognition*.[40] The main findings of this paper are based on a survey conducted of 1408 middle school and high school students in the US on their study strategy preferences and reactions to a classroom-based program of retrieval practice. The results showed that: 'For classes in which retrieval practice occurred, 92% of students reported that retrieval practice helped them learn and 72% reported that retrieval practice made them less nervous for unit tests and exams.' The authors also added, 'in light of our results, we encourage K-12 teachers to use retrieval practice in their classrooms to reduce test anxiety and improve learning'.

Bush and Watson, also comment on the issue of retrieval practice and anxiety in their book. They conclude that: 'The message to students couldn't be clearer or simpler: don't study in order to do well at the test. Do lots of tests in order to do well. By doing so, they will learn more and perform better under pressure.'[41]

I think the way we as teachers approach retrieval practice in the classroom is essential to how it is perceived by our students. This can depend on the language and terminology we use from test, assessment to quiz or task. Another factor can be how regular we embed retrieval practice into our lessons, once it becomes part of a classroom routine it normalises this strategy. Also, the points Sherrington made, such as specifying the knowledge and varying the diet, can also help greatly with students embracing retrieval practice as a learning strategy. The retrieval tasks in the book have been well received by my classes as

40. Agarwal, P. K., D'Antonio, L., Roediger, H. L., McDermott, K. B. and McDaniel, M. A. (2014) 'Classroom-based programs of retrieval practice reduce middle school and high school students' test anxiety', *Journal of Applied Research in Memory and Cognition* 3 (3) pp. 131-139.
41. Busch, B. and Watson, E. (2019) *The Science of Learning. 77 Studies That Every Teacher Needs to Know.* Abingdon, Oxon: Routledge, p. 157.

they are very enjoyable and fun for my students – two words not often associated with the testing effect!

Agarwal writes on her brilliant website (www.retrievelearn.com) how we as educators can flip the narrative with retrieval practice from a negative and anxiety provoking test to a positive strategy that will increase confidence and success. Below are her four recommendations:

1. 'Start a discussion about how we use retrieval in everyday life – thinking about what we did last weekend, remembering a quote from a favourite movie, etc. Ask students: Do these types of retrieval activities feel negative? Do they make you anxious? Why not?

2. Emphasise that retrieval in the classroom is similar to retrieval outside the classroom. Drawing on students' explanations from the first point helps draw this parallel. When retrieval is no-stakes, we can learn from our experiences without consequences.

3. Acknowledge that the process of retrieval can feel challenging. This is a good thing for learning! Retrieval is a "desirable difficulty" that has large benefits down the road.

4. Explain that, based on decades of research, retrieval practice helps students learn more and learn longer. This means that students may study outside of class less because they're remembering more of what they learned during class.'[42]

Dr Megan Sumeracki and Dr Yana Weinstein have pointed out that 'to gain the most benefit, students do need to successfully retrieve a certain amount of the information during retrieval practice. Imagine if a student just stared at a blank sheet of paper and could not remember anything about what they had just read; this would be unlikely to produce learning',[43] plus consider the implications on their morale and confidence. Therefore, retrieval success can be a very positive factor and motivator for students.

Retrieval practice has also helped my confidence as a teacher. The exam period can be stressful for teachers too but regular retrieval and spaced practice ensures content and skills have been revised and retrieved regularly so our students are better prepared for their exams and whilst my exam nerves never disappeared, I did feel better as a result of these strategies.

42. Agarwal, P. K. (2019) 'Weekly Teaching Tips', *Retrieval Practice* [Online]. Retrieved from: www.bit.ly/2WMhXoy
43. Sumeracki, M. A. and Weinstein, Y. (2018) 'Optimising learning using retrieval practice', *Impact* 2 pp. 13-16.

Is retrieval practice deemed more effective for older students?

As a secondary teacher, with classes at GCSE and A Level, retrieval practice has become an essential part of my classroom planning and delivery. Is retrieval practice as relevant and helpful in a primary or middle school setting? Firstly, and anecdotally – as I mentioned already – I did introduce retrieval practice and other areas of the science of learning to many of my students. I spent a considerable amount of time doing so. In 2016 I had GCSE and A Level classes that I would teach for the next two years, both classes were small and consisted of very hardworking and motivated learners.

I found the students in my Year 10 class were much more welcoming and receptive of these strategies in comparison to my Year 12 class. The main reason for this I believe was that the Year 10 students were beginning their GCSE course and preparing for an external examination that they had not done before. Year 12 were more reluctant in regards to embracing evidence-informed techniques. The majority of the students in my Year 12 class had achieved very good results at GCSE using techniques such as re-reading and highlighting, therefore they felt confident that those strategies worked for them and they should carry on using those tried and tested techniques, thus ignoring my advice about retrieval practice. If highlighting and re-reading worked then why change now? This was a general attitude towards this new research they were finding out about.

My Year 12 class had answered past exam papers, both inside and outside of class, in addition to self-testing to support their revision, so they were using retrieval practice as a study strategy they just weren't aware of it. The Year 12 students told me they had dedicated hours and hours across days, weeks and months to their revision whilst others admitted to cramming previously. What if there were strategies students could use that meant they would not have to spend as long revising to learn material – wouldn't that be amazing? Cue the science of learning!

It was a different experience teaching my Year 10 class, a class that fully embraced retrieval practice, spaced practice, dual coding and more in comparison with the Year 12s, who clearly didn't enjoy the regular quizzing and much preferred strategies I was trying to move away from.

The majority of students eventually embraced these strategies but it was challenging at times with my Year 12 class and I had to be very resilient with retrieval practice. Two years later, the students from my original Year 10 class had begun their A Level courses. I didn't need to explain the science of learning as they were very familiar with a wide range of techniques that they had used in history lessons and had also applied to other subjects. They had developed evidence-informed and effective study habits and routines that they could now use and apply at A Level with ease.

The students in that cohort fully understood why lessons began with retrieval practice and appreciated how this technique would identify the gaps in their knowledge for them to act on. The sooner we educate our students with this valuable information the better! I was teaching my Year 12 students a very demanding and content-heavy A Level course in addition to educating them on the science of learning. They were initially reluctant to accept the research because it was unfamiliar and out of their comfort zone, but it would have been even better if they too were beginning their A Level course with the knowledge and understanding of the power of effective learning and revision strategies.

That's just an example of my experience. What does the research say about retrieval practice and age? Dunlosky has already been quoted in this book for suggesting that the most effective strategies work for learners of all ages. There is also a paper that addresses this question focusing on this question: 'Retrieval-Based Learning: Positive Effects of Retrieval Practice in Elementary School Children' by Jeffrey D. Karpicke and Megan Sumeracki.[44] They pointed out that a lot of 'research has demonstrated that practicing retrieval is a powerful way to enhance learning. However, nearly all prior research has examined retrieval practice with college students. Little is known about retrieval practice in children, and even less is known about possible individual differences in retrieval practice.'

They conducted a study with three experiments, involving 88 children with a mean age of ten years, who studied a list of words and either re-studied the words or practiced retrieving them. Students then took a final free recall or recognition test. In the different experiments, children showed robust retrieval practice effects. The research also found that some tasks that worked well with college/university students were not as effective with younger students, which is perhaps not surprising as we know primary, secondary and further education teachers will plan and deliver lessons differently and accordingly. Sumeracki has observed that: 'It seems that in order for retrieval practice to work well with students of any age, we need to ensure that students are successful in the recall activity.'

---

44. Karpicke, J. D. and Sumeracki, M. (2006) 'Retrieval-Based Learning: Positive Effects of Retrieval Practice in Elementary School Children', *Frontiers in Psychology* 7 (104) pp. 1-9.

Sumeracki further adds, 'retrieval practice works well for students of many ages and abilities but, for some students, writing out everything they know on a blank sheet of paper may be a daunting task that does not lead to much successful retrieval. To increase success, teachers can implement scaffolded retrieval tasks [...] with scaffolding, the students can successfully produce the information and work their way up to recalling the information on their own.' Sumeracki also comments that: 'Scaffolding is a great way to help increase retrieval success. Scaffolding could be implemented with any student, but it may be particularly important with students who may struggle to recall on their own from the start.'[45]

I am aware of a contradiction here, as I have previously discussed the importance of retrieval practice without notes or support, but Sumeracki is referring explicitly to younger students. Also, a combination of retrieval strategies are ideal in the classroom, therefore some techniques may include support (not too much as this will reduce retrieval effort) combined with opportunities for free recall without support. It's a balance we find in our classrooms based on the content we have taught, the stage in the learning process and through knowing our classes well. I am hopeful many, if not all, of the tasks in this book can be used and adapted by primary and middle school teachers to support retrieval in their classrooms.

Is retrieval practice regarded as effective for students of all abilities?

I saw this question posed online and I think it is an interesting point to consider. I teach mixed ability classes in a non-selective school and I have been using retrieval practice with all of my students and classes (linked to the point above about involving everyone and providing retrieval opportunities for all).

The paper 'Test-Enhanced Learning in the Classroom: Long-Term Improvements From Quizzing' states: 'Our research demonstrates that retrieval practice benefits both low and high ability students. Because retrieval practice is a simple, flexible learning strategy, it can be adapted to a wide variety of situations, including special education and gifted classrooms. Further, students can practice retrieval at home (e.g. answering practice questions, using flash cards) or in the classroom (e.g. with low-stakes quizzing). In other words, retrieval practice isn't just a teaching strategy; it's a powerful study strategy, too.'[46]

45. Firth, J., Smith, M., Harvard, B. and Boxer, A. (2017) 'Assessment as learning: The role of retrieval practice in the classroom', *Impact* [Online] September. Retrieved from: www.bit.ly/35H5JBY
46. Roediger, H. L., Agarwal, P. K., McDaniel, M. A. and McDermott, K. B. (2011) 'Test-Enhanced Learning in the Classroom: Long-Term Improvement From Quizzing', *Journal of Experimental Psychology Applied* 17 (4) pp. 382–395.

This confirming what I had already assumed. My advice for retrieval with SEN students – although individual contexts apply here – is to provide support with the process and ensure the task design is clear and very straightforward so that working memory does not become overloaded.

My experience as a teacher in an international British curriculum school, working with a lot of 'English as an Additional Language' students (EAL), has shown that regular retrieval tasks designed to supported vocabulary instruction are very beneficial for EAL learners. It provides lots of recall opportunities and repeated exposure to subject-specific terminology in a variety of different contexts. The majority of the retrieval tasks can be adapted to focus on vocabulary, not just definitions but spellings, pronunciation, etymology and application and transfer of key terms in different contexts.

Retrieval practice: Should we use recognition, free recall or both?

This is a very interesting question that I have considered and reflected on in recent years. It may seem that there is conflicting advice as to whether retrieval practice should involve no or little support but context is key and this answer is slightly complex. I use regular multiple-choice quizzing but there is a lot of research that say students benefit more from answering questions that don't provide any cues, clues or ask students to select the correct answer, although we should consider the point Sumeracki made that younger students need some support and scaffolding to aid their retrieval. The fantastic work of Dunlosky *et al* also illustrated that tests or quizzes that require recall from memory will be more effective for developing long-term memory. This is not to dismiss multiple-choice quizzing, as it can be a useful form of daily review and can be of a varied retrieval diet.

Multiple-choice quizzes involve the process of recognition as students have to simply identify the correct answer. This is easier than recalling it without any support, however there are various benefits of using multiple-choice quizzes. Quiz questions that require short answers will need the teacher to check answers, unlike the majority of quizzing apps which do that automatically with multiple-choice questions. Free recall quizzes will be more time consuming for the teacher to assess but the reason short answers are more beneficial than answering a multiple-choice question is that it simply requires more effort from the student.

To answer the question and conclude: research has suggested teachers should combine the two methods of recognition with multiple-choice quizzing and free recall. This is because multiple-choice quizzing often leads to greater retrieval success than short answer questions with free recall (in addition to supporting teacher workload, resulting in more regular retrieval opportunities). The benefits of retrieval practice can depend on both the retrieval difficulty and retrieval success, so combining the harder questions with opportunities for success would be optimal.

Are there any negative effects or downsides to retrieval practice?

The reading and research about retrieval practice is overwhelmingly positive. It is widely recognised and accepted as an effective learning strategy. The low or no stakes aspect has meant that this strategy hasn't received a negative backlash in comparison to the formal qualifications and testing that are currently used to measure students progress, attainment and ability. I have fully embraced and welcomed retrieval practice, but I still thought this was an important question to include and consider to show how teachers can be reflective and critical consumers of educational research.

The research paper focusing on the ten benefits of testing also addresses criticisms too but the authors were able to persuade that the benefits outweighed the possible negative consequences. The issues raised by critics included the negative impact of regular retrieval practice on classroom time, the comparisons to rote learning with 'drill and kill' (something I will discuss later in the book) and the retrieval–induced forgetting – focusing on some aspects but not all could result in forgetting other material not tested.

Another criticism that has been continually raised is that a lot of the experiments carried out that focused on the 'testing effect' were not done in classroom conditions. This has been recognised by academic researchers and Karpicke addressed this: 'Our aim in the experiments reported here was to investigate the testing effect under educationally relevant conditions, using prose materials and free recall tests without feedback (somewhat akin to essay tests used in education).' Various experiments carried out in an educational context have replicated the results that testing is a powerful method of learning.[47]

The studies I have referenced in this book have carried out experiments on sample sizes and in certain conditions and we need to consider would it be exactly the same in other contexts with different participants? We simply don't know. Various studies have replicated similar results showing that there is a strong supporting corpus of research to support the efficacy of

---

47. Karpicke, J. D. (2012) 'Retrieval-Based Learning: Active Retrieval Promotes Meaningful Learning', *Current Directions in Psychological Science* 21 (3) pp. 157-163.

retrieval practice. However, in psychology the research is highly complex and there are so many factors to be considered.

Anecdotally, I can think of one specific example where retrieval practice led to a student disengaging with learning. A conscientious and hardworking student confided in me that they chose not to study a specific subject at A Level because the teacher had used the same style retrieval quiz every lesson for two years at GCSE. I did explain to the student about how A Level choices should not be based on the teacher or activities but their decision had been made. The student understood why the teacher was continually using retrieval practice every lesson, as many other teachers were doing so but the student felt the retrieval quizzes were often far too difficult and mundane. Eventually this created a sense of dread approaching the lessons because it felt more like constant testing than quizzing, despite the lack of high stakes.

The lesson always began with a simple and clear knowledge test – referred to as knowledge tests – which, once again, link back to the importance of language and terminology. If a quiz is low or no stakes, but still referred to as a test, then the connotations of testing and exams can still exist. In regards to difficulty, Brown *et al* stated that for a task to be desirable the level of difficulty must be something that learners can overcome through increased effort.[48] If students feel that achieving a goal is unlikely or unrealistic, then they will give up and this is undesirable, as shown in this example.

This example of repetitive testing in the same format every lesson also links back to Sherrington's point about variety, mixing it up. Lessons could always begin with retrieval practice, but the type of quiz and activity could be rotated and changed on a regular basis. Clearly, the teacher had good intentions, was evidence informed and carrying out regular knowledge tests to ensure their students can retrieve information and be successful in the GCSE examinations. However, this strategy had a negative effect on the learner because of the retrieval difficulty, lack of opportunities for retrieval success and the repetitive nature of the task.

Dan Rodriguez-Clark, a maths teacher in an international school has reflected that planning retrieval practice can be hard, in regards to scheduling how to space the retrieval, which addresses an issue with combining retrieval and spaced practice. I agree that combining retrieval

---

48. Brown, P. C., Roediger, H. L. and McDaniel, M. A. (2014) *Make It Stick: The Science of Successful Learning.* Cambridge, MA: Harvard Education Press, p. 99.

and spaced practice certainly does require thought, consideration and careful planning, this is why it is vital teachers are provided with time to implement retrieval practice into their planning and practice. He also adds that some teachers view retrieval practice as simply a quiz, failing to build it into lessons but instead focusing on one-off isolated activities.

Simon Beale, teacher and leader, has commented that the 'low-stakes nature of retrieval practice can make students feel like it's acceptable to keep on getting it wrong without ever putting in the effort to get it right'. Therefore, without any pressure or stakes, students might not try as hard as they would in comparison to a test that could be recorded or reported back to parents. Although Beale wasn't referring to all students, this is a really interesting point and he further added, 'it can be followed up and addressed, of course, but once you start monitoring and recording quizzes it isn't low-stakes anymore'. We need students to understand that low or no stakes doesn't equate to 'no effort', but instead retrieval practice is an important learning strategy that they should take seriously. We need our students to become invested in retrieval practice and that can be hard to achieve initially.

Many other teachers have told me that they struggle to find time for retrieval activities, especially with the pressures of exam classes and content. I can fully understand these points and my advice would be to persevere and ensure that retrieval time is built into lessons because it will be worth it in the long term, especially with those exam classes too. It is worth reflecting how we spend time in the classroom instead of trying to add retrieval to lessons; let's reflect on what do in the lesson and focus on making it as efficient and effective as possible. A suggestion would be to remove the plenary task from the end of a lesson and use it as a retrieval task next lesson or at a later date.

It is an effective strategy with many benefits that outweigh the negative points, but no strategy is perfect or all encompassing, and we should know now, after many years of searching and failing, that there is simply no silver bullet in education, not even retrieval practice.

Why the sudden interest in retrieval practice now?

You may have noticed the dates of research referenced in the book so far showing when the research was conducted or recorded, and find yourself shocked to be reading a book published in 2019 that is referencing research from 1885, the 1950s and '60s, in addition to many journals and studies carried out within the last 20 years. The research into memory and cognitive psychology has been taking place for over a century. I have been teaching for nine years now, but only engaging with educational research for half of that time.

I was surprised to read the dates of the research I have been reading because, if this information has been available for so long, why was this not featured as part of my initial teacher training in 2010? Why has it taken so long to become mainstream in education? Where has this sudden resurgence of interest in cognitive psychology come from?

Researchers and academics with knowledge of memory and retrieval practice have also felt frustration at the slow pace it has taken for this information to reach teachers and learners. Karpicke wrote in 2012: 'Given the fundamental importance of retrieval for understanding the process of learning, it is surprising that retrieval processes have not received more attention in educational research.'[49] In the same paper he argued that 'retrieval is often not granted the central role it deserves', but I do think retrieval practice is finally moving towards receiving that recognition, focus and attention it deserves.

I think there have been a few reasons for this, which I have already made a brief reference to, but I will expand on those points further. Firstly, I think Twitter should be credited as a marvellous channel for connecting teachers, leaders and academic researchers. Through Twitter I have been able to follow experts in this field from Paul Kirschner, Pedro De Bruyckere, `the Learning Scientists and many more. I've also been able to follow other educators that are sharing information and blogging about retrieval practice in their classrooms.

Another reason is due to the ResearchED movement founded by Tom Bennett and assisted by Hélène Galdin-O'Shea. ResearchEd – for anyone that isn't aware of this phenomenon in education – is a grassroots organisation that aims to raise research literacy in education and it has been growing rapidly since 2013. ResearchEd events are always very well attended and combine presentations from leading experts such as Dylan Wiliam, Daniel Willingham and more, in addition to providing educators with the opportunity to share how research has had an impact on their practice.

I felt very fortunate to attend and present at ResearchEd Dubai in 2019, reflecting how the call for change that started in the UK is now a global movement! I believe ResearchEd will continue to fight the good fight, debunking absurd neuromyths that haunt education, and ensure that cognitive psychology and other areas of research don't fall victim to

49. Karpicke, J. D. (2012) 'Retrieval-Based Learning: Active Retrieval Promotes Meaningful Learning', *Current Direction in Psychological Science* 21 (3) pp. 157-163.

flavour of the month, disappearing to a new fad, but instead remain at the forefront of teaching and learning.

There's now an increasing choice of educational books that educators can read which focus on educational research. There has been criticism that this market has become saturated and it can be difficult, or even intimidating, to try to keep up with the regular release and publication of books. It is important teachers don't feel overwhelmed and that reading does become an integral part of our professional learning without adding to already challenging workloads. My only point in response to people complaining about there being too many educational books is to realise that we don't *have* to purchase and read them all – we have the power to be selective. I think it is better to have too many books about education than too few. The choice of books available is ultimately a good thing.

Many schools are now investing in CPD libraries for their staff to promote a reading culture (I think teachers should ask about this in an interview: 'Does your school have a CPD library?', 'What books are included?' and 'If not, then why?'). I am sure as you read this book you will notice that I reference and credit many other educational books. I do make time for reading books but this will entirely depend on my workload and priorities, as no doubt it will be the same for other teachers. I really do enjoy reading educational books and it certainly doesn't feel like a chore or something I am forced to do, which seems to be a common sentiment shared amongst educators.

Finally, the accessibility of information about retrieval practice has become – and continues to be – very easy and practical for busy teachers. Pooja Agarwal is referenced in this book for the research she has carried out and the book she has authored with teacher Patrice Baine, but in addition to that she has set up a website dedicated to retrieval practice with free downloads for teachers and students that include guides written by cognitive scientists and resources. You can find out more if you visit www.retrievalpractice.org

There is also a vast amount of material online to support teachers including Seneca Learning: www.app.senecalearning.com. All that is required is an email address to create an account. There are lots of courses available on this site, for both teachers and students, but the specific course I recommend is the 'Cognitive Science for Teachers – Seneca Certified Educator'.

There is a free course and it covers a range of topics linked to cognitive psychology, such as: different types of memory, how we learn, cognitive load theory and effective classroom strategies. The user works their way through the course and you can always stop and resume it at a later point. Once the online learner has read the material/slides they answer a series of questions based on that content. If you are a classroom teacher or leader this is very useful. If you are a middle or senior leader then you could share this with your colleagues and discuss the course together at a later stage, once completed.

Case study: Engaging, embracing and embedding educational research

When I was in Hong Kong at AISC 2018 I attended a workshop led by four teachers that are based in an international school in Kuala Lumpur. During their workshop the teachers shared a range of practical ideas and resources they had collated for attendees to take away and implement. They also collectively explained how they have welcomed educational research and outlined the strategies they have used to further develop their own professional learning collaboratively.

I remember listening to this group of teachers and thinking to myself how much I would love to work with them. Their enthusiasm, energy and excitement for the science of learning was infectious and evident for all in the audience to see. Alexandra Gordon was one of the teachers that presented and delivered this workshop. She is a science teacher and head of Year 11 and through Twitter I have been fortunate to remain in contact with her. I wanted her to share her passion and professional learning journey in this book as a way to inspire others and show teachers and leaders how this can be achieved in a school environment.

> I love learning; especially learning about learning as I feel that teaching is a career that never stands still. Despite a great professional learning programme with professional learning communities (PLC) at my current school, I felt there were teachers within my school that would enjoy and benefit from reading more educational texts (myself included, there is no doubt that the book club was created and grew out of my own selfish reasons).

> I set up a school book club as a voluntary group. We meet one morning a week with a cup of tea and decide on a text to read, varying from journal articles, blogs and books to exploring educational websites. The following week we feedback our thoughts, anything we loved, ideas it has sparked that we can take into our teaching practice and, of course, parts that we perhaps disagreed with, which has triggered some great debates and discussions.

> Through the book club we discovered 'The Learning Scientists' and their blog www.learningscientists.org. Instantly we were intrigued with

the content on their site and we wanted to find out more. Over the next few months this led to more reading around retrieval practice, but as I developed the book club as a forum for all types of reading, I didn't want to focus on one aspect of teaching in too much detail.

Therefore, the 'Learning Strategies' PLC was born. This was a more formal group, which staff opted into. Aims were discussed with the intention of developing this as part of our teaching practice. We began researching retrieval practice, the science behind it and practical strategies we could trial in our classrooms. From there we went away and did just that, trialling different activities to gain insight about what worked for us in our classroom contexts.

The meetings that followed consisted of feeding back what worked well and any issues that were encountered. Discussions allowed everyone to develop their ideas and go away wanting to trial more. By the end of the year every teacher in the PLC had successfully embedded at least one new learning strategy into his or her practice, not just focusing on retrieval.

Along this journey the opportunity to present at AISC in Hong Kong came along. I spoke to some regular attendees of the book club and asked if they would like to run a workshop together. The following week we submitted a proposal, we were accepted and began planning our session. We were overjoyed by the reception we received. The positive comments from everyone who attended encouraged us to continue working together. We created a website which we add to and update as we learn more and reflect. We have also led whole school inset on this topic and ran a similar workshop at the Association of International Malaysian Schools conference in Kuala Lumpur.

By embracing educational research and professional learning, I have continued to grow as an educator and learner in the same way I expect my students to.

You can follow Alexandra Gordon on Twitter @pedagogygeek

Alexandra has demonstrated what I believe all great teachers have in common. There are many attributes and qualities that great teachers possess, but ultimately all great teachers never stop learning. I am a strong advocate for teachers taking ownership of their own professional development and learning because doing so improved my own teaching practice and many aspects of my life. Taking responsibility of your own professional development will enhance and perhaps, eventually, transform your teaching practice.

Whilst there are many challenges facing the teaching profession currently from the retention crisis to workload issues, funding and mental health problems – to name just a few of the main topics dominating global headlines – I also think it is a very exciting time to be a teacher. In recent years, professional learning has been reinvigorated. Professional development is now much more accessible and enjoyable than ever before. Educators around the world have shown that they are leading the way, with ownership of their own professional development and learning.

I have created an infographic in figure 4 with six suggested methods of professional learning for all educators showing the different ways we can embrace and reflect on research and practice.

Figure 4 Methods of professional learning for teachers and leaders

Case study: Practitioner research into retrieval practice – The British School Al Khubairat (BSAK) Abu Dhabi, UAE

I feel very privileged and grateful to be working alongside colleagues and senior leaders that are all very keen to learn more, develop as professionals and are ultimately driven by the desire to improve outcomes for the students at our school. Nigel Davis, Deputy Headteacher, responsible for teaching and learning at BSAK, clearly leads by example in all that he does. Nigel and I have had many interesting conversations and reflections about retrieval practice. In the 2019/2020 academic year, the school has four key areas of focus: literacy, feedback, questioning and cognitive science.

Nigel is an advocate and enthusiast of practitioner research, combining this with his own reading and reflections. To do this Nigel and the geography department at BSAK chose to focus on the impact of retrieval practice as a starter task and the impact this had on learners in the classroom. Below Nigel summarises how he did this and what the results illustrated:

Like many teachers and leaders over the past few years, I have read, with increasing interest and joy, the improving volume of resources and information about how students learn. Cognitive science is clearly impacting on our practice as professionals. I truly believe that the best schools, and the best teachers, are embedding the clear ideas of retrieval practice, metacognition, dual coding and many others into their working lives, for the benefit of our students' learning.

However, the issue I had back in 2018 was just that – 'I believe' it is having a huge effect. I was not, and could not, be sure. Mark Twain once said that: 'In religion and politics, people's beliefs and convictions are in almost every case gotten at secondhand and without examination'. This so easily applies to education today, as Paul Kirschner has highlighted. EduTwitter, blogs and podcasts are all amazing, they are a brilliant soapbox and sharing platform for our profession, but we choose to implement things that we see as 'making sense' (and, as Kate puts it, quite rightly the things we believe will have 'low effort, high impact'). The trouble with this is that the evidence sometimes shows that the greatest impacts on learning are not necessarily the ones that make the most sense. It struck me that I wanted to prove to myself that there was merit in what I believed would work.

So I set about creating a randomised trial within the BSAK geography department. I am no researcher: outside of my undergraduate geography degree and a MA in education dissertations, I had never completed any research before and I am certainly no trained cognitive scientist. I also realised that the small scale of the trial meant that the validity of my trial outside of our department was questionable, although I am confident that any findings we discovered would be transferable to schools in a similar context. I also felt that we were in a very fortunate position at my school – one of the leading schools in the Middle East, with enthusiastic and compliant students who were used to 'giving things a go'; in effect, a relatively 'clean' teaching laboratory, where results from any trial have a higher than normal chance of being down to the impact of the change.

So I set about completing this piece of practitioner research: investigating the impact on student outcomes of a planned series of retrieval practice tasks at the start of lessons, when compared with non-retrieval-based starters. We completed this research using a Year 9 scheme of work on desert environments, which lasted for nine lessons, spread over six weeks.

I endeavoured to produce a randomised control trial experiment with our Year 9 cohort. The cohort is split into two half-year groups (X and Y), with three groups of mixed ability students in each half of the year group. I had a semblance of a baseline for each half, with both CAT4 scores on cognitive ability, and the previous terms teacher assessed attainment, both of which showed slightly higher scores for the Y band than the X band.

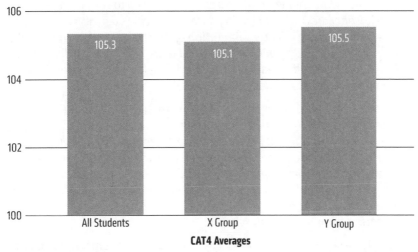

Figure 5 CAT4 averages

The students also completed a baseline test at the start of the course, to see how much prior knowledge they had of desert environments. The baseline test was also broken down into knowledge, understanding and skills sections, as I thought it would be interesting to see if there were particular areas of geography that benefitted from retrieval practice more than others. The areas also provided evidence that the Y side of the year group were at a higher starting point than the X band, having a higher initial test average score. The understanding score for the Y band was the clearest difference, being much higher than the X band. Interestingly, the knowledge score was the same for both sides.

I randomly chose X to receive the retrieval starters. The band Y classes received starters that challenged them to think about the topic they would be learning about this lesson, a 'hook' style starter. There were starter tasks that I had been using for years, that are geared towards 'warming up the brain', engaging the students in the topic at hand and developing softer skills such as discussions, listening skills, thinking and creativity. Both starter types were designed to last for around 15 minutes of a 55-minute lesson.

Apart from the starters, everything else was taught in exactly the same way. We use schemes of work within our department that give detailed lesson plans to ensure consistency, while every teacher has the autonomy to tailor their lesson to the needs of their groups, as well as for the ability to delve wider into a topic if they felt it benefits learning – a 'tight but loose' methodology for lesson preparation. However, for the purposes of this trial, each lesson was designed with greater detail and staff were asked to stick to the details of each lesson plan. Although having different teachers delivering the lessons to different groups was clearly a limitation of the study, the three geography teachers were split evenly between the two bands, and our knowledge of the staff is that they are all excellent teachers, who all have a record for producing startlingly good results with their GCSE and A Level classes.

The retrieval-based starter varied each lesson in their design. I do feel that when teaching, too much of the same thing can be damaging to the engagement of the students, so I resisted the temptation of having the students complete the same type of retrieval starter. For the purposes of this trial, I also avoided digging into students' longer term memory by interleaving past topics' recall. Although this is a practice I would now use, I felt that for the purposes of this trial, I should only focus on retrieving information from the current scheme.

The retrieval starter tasks were relatively simple as the aim was to ensure that the students were delving into their memory banks to retrieve some knowledge, apply the knowledge to understanding, and to practise some of the skills that they had learned in previous lessons. I had some favourites – the competitive nature of the retrieval grids and a 'noughts and crosses' style task engaged the students well. I really think that the 'if this is the answer, what is the question' task makes students consider their understanding and knowledge in a different way, so I felt that this was a huge success.

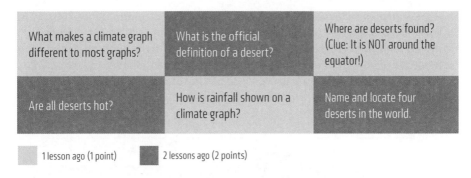

What makes a climate graph different to most graphs?	What is the official definition of a desert?	Where are deserts found? (Clue: It is NOT around the equator!)
Are all deserts hot?	How is rainfall shown on a climate graph?	Name and locate four deserts in the world.

1 lesson ago (1 point)   2 lessons ago (2 points)

Figure 6 Retrieval Grid: Deserts Lesson 3

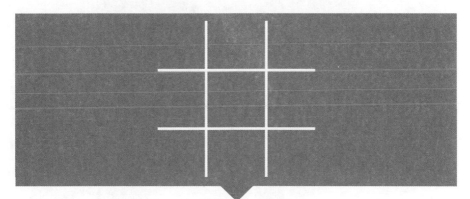

We will play noughts and crosses: working in pairs, draw the grid above into the back of one person's book. Number 1 goes first – they are playing noughts (0). They can put a 0 anywhere they want IF they get their first question correct!

Figure 7 Noughts and crosses

At the end of the scheme of work, the final lesson was an unannounced test. This was indeed exactly the same test that they had been given in lesson 1. I hoped that by doing this, we could really see if the difference in the teaching method had made any difference to the students' progress. As figure 8 shows – there certainly was an impressive difference in the results. In particular, figures 9 and 10 show a far better improvement in knowledge and understanding results.

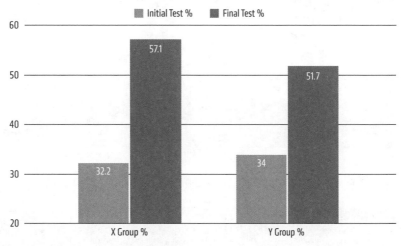

Figure 8 Differences in tests 1 and 2 for each band

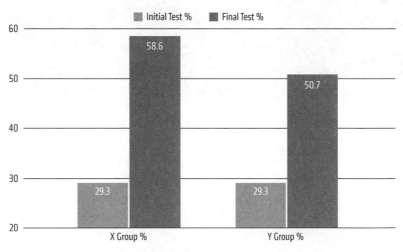

Figure 9 Knowledge section improvements

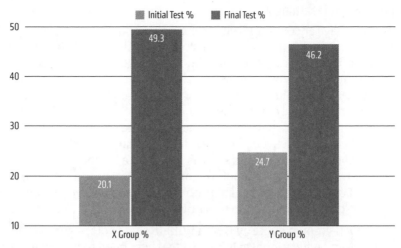

Figure 10 Understanding section improvements

Although I would love to have discovered that retrieval practice was a panacea for low ability students to bridge the gap in their learning, unfortunately, in this research it seemed to indicate the opposite. It showed that the greatest progress was made by students in the higher ability group, perhaps emphasising that their schemas were made stronger to their wider base knowledge.

Finally, what did the students think? Feedback was positive, although some students did give a groan of 'retrieval again?'. On reflection, calling each starter 'Let's Retrieve' was a mistake. As we started the next scheme, however, students were asking about doing more retrieval, as they could really see the benefits.

In summary, I was able to demonstrate that within geography classrooms at BSAK the use of retrieval practice for starters made a significant difference to the long-term memory of our students. It has certainly changed our practice for the better, and although not every lesson starts with retrieval, certainly most do (and this now includes interleaving past interconnected learning too) – and, unlike in 2018, I can now say with confidence that 'I know' it will be making a difference!

You can follow Nigel Davis on Twitter @BSAKT&L

The professional learning gap

A difficulty I have encountered when writing this book was where to pitch some of the information, research and content. I address this because I know many educators are very familiar with working memory, the forgetting curve and so on. However, I still meet teachers on a regular basis that are not familiar with the terms or research behind retrieval practice and the science of learning. Since announcing the publication of this book many teachers have contacted me and the comments ranged from, 'I don't know much about retrieval practice so I'm hoping your book will help me' to other comments such as 'I've read a lot about retrieval practice for many years so I'm looking forward to learning a lot more from your book'. I certainly hope that this book will benefit everyone reading it, whether you consider yourself to be a novice or expert.

There is a well-known quote by Dylan Wiliam that is often shared at conferences and educational events: 'All teachers need to improve their practice – not because they are not good enough, but because they can be better.' This is a really important message that all teachers should take notice of.

The professional learning gap is how I describe this and that gap is widening. This isn't good for the profession in addition to bringing many challenges for both teachers and leaders. There are many teachers that are very knowledgeable about the latest developments in education and are actively taking ownership of their professional learning. This can be achieved by the different methods suggested in this chapter to stay informed as the profession moves forward.

In the opposite camp are teachers who are reluctant to engage and develop professionally or have perhaps plateaued, with no interest or responsibility for their own professional learning, which is very disappointing. I have sympathy with teachers that struggle to find the time to engage with research or reading, that is not what I am referring to (hopefully workload issues will change and leaders can be more supportive of this), but the teachers that have the notion that they don't need to keep learning and developing is not the right attitude we should model to our students.

After reading an educational book that I found interesting I recommended it to a head of department that I know as some suggested reading. I offered to loan my copy for them to read. This individual was very dismissive and turned down my offer; they told me that their results were consistently exceptional and they had always been rated as an 'Outstanding' teacher from lesson observations throughout their career, so there really was no need in reading any books or blogs as an attempt to improve. Do you know anyone like this? This is clearly not the right outlook or approach to learning, whether you are a classroom teacher or leader.

There are teachers who are engaging with research and evidence yet they feel frustrated because senior leaders at their schools are not doing so. In contrast to that are the senior and middle leaders that are leading by example, being evidence informed, but struggle to motivate their colleagues to do the same. I don't have the answers for this and I am sure a professional learning gap will always exist, as it likely does in all other professions, but the fact that you are reading this book shows you are dedicating time to develop your professional learning.

Summary

- There are a lot more benefits to retrieval practice than just remembering facts.

- It is clear that retrieval practice is a better study strategy than other popular techniques such as highlighting and re-reading.

- Variety is key: retrieval practice doesn't have to be repetitive testing. It can be stimulating, challenging and enjoyable.

- It has never been easier or more accessible to find out and learn more about retrieval practice, this can be achieved through blogs, books, podcasts and at events.

- The professional learning gap is getting wider as more educators are learning and developing at a rapid pace in comparison to other educators who are reluctant to do so.

Recommended reading

Rosenshine's Principles in Action by Tom Sherrington

The Science of Learning: 77 Studies That Every Teacher Needs to Know by Bradley Bush and Edward Watson

The Ingredients for Great Teaching by Pedro De Bruyckere

Make It Stick: The Science of Successful Learning by Peter C. Brown, Henry L. Roediger III, Mark A. McDaniel

Why Don't Students Like School? A Cognitive Scientist Answers Questions About How the Mind Works and What It Means for the Classroom by Daniel Willingham

CHAPTER 2: RETRIEVAL PRACTICE IN THE CLASSROOM

Understanding the research around retrieval practice is important but it is only half of the piece of the retrieval practice puzzle because it needs to be implemented and embedded in the classroom to ensure impact. In the previous chapter I wanted to unpick and share my reflections on the research I have read that has influenced my practice but this is the chapter where I feel more at home – so to speak – writing about teaching and learning in the classroom.

The key questions teachers keep coming back to when reading and reflecting on educational research are: 'What does this look like in my classroom?' and 'How can I apply it to my classroom?' Again, I hope this chapter, filled with practical examples that can be adapted across subjects and key stages, will help greatly with this.

Retrieval practice placemat

Placemats are easy to create and use, especially my example in figure 1 as you can print it and use it in your classroom immediately, or you can adapt mine and create your own. Laminating the placemats will ensure they last longer in your classroom or alternatively as a paperless option you could simply project the placemat onto the board as a slide for students to read and discuss. I have found this to be a more convenient option as I am not always based in the same classroom.

The aim of my retrieval practice placemat is to promote verbal discussions amongst peers about previous content covered, as well as retrieve that information from their memories by doing so.

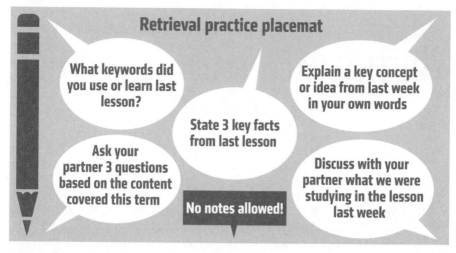

Figure 1 Retrieval practice placemat

When I created this resource I was initially concerned about how generic it is; I felt that perhaps students needed at least some cues. I contacted teacher and blogger Blake Harvard via Twitter to ask for some advice.

This led to a very interesting discussion and prompted Blake to write about this type of resource. This is what Blake wrote about the retrieval practice placemat and why he thinks it is an effective resource for the classroom:

- **All of the tasks are quite generalised.** They can be applied across a multitude of subjects and ability levels.

- **The laissez-faire nature of the tasks.** This may be my favourite point. Notice how there's very little subject-specific 'help' from the question to assist the learner, forcing the student to recall all of the information. When designing my own reviews for my students, I try to remember that I don't want the question doing the cognitive work for the students. Provide the framework for answering the question, but allow the student to do all of the domain-specific work. Learning is effortful.

- **The potential for quality study habits to be formed.** If students can keep these general questioning prompts in their mind, they can always be used for study/practice, no matter the subject. This questioning is much better for providing feedback to the students and for retention of material than simply re-reading or highlighting their notes.

- **It is simple.** Learning doesn't have to be complicated. I think, in general, many of the 'innovative' stuff we are doing today only complicates the classroom. We should aim to make the classroom simpler. I will certainly use this in my classroom. It provides the students with many different opportunities to retrieve important material, it provides an opportunity for students to assess what they know and what they don't know, and it reinforces more efficient and effective study/practice habits.

Blake raises a lot of valid points that I hadn't considered. Placemats are not new in education, they have been used in the classroom to support literacy and independence, but I adapted this versatile resource to support retrieval practice in the classroom. Are there any of your existing resources that could be tweaked and adapted to be used as a retrieval practice exercise as I did with my placemat?

You can read more of Blake's reflections and thought-provoking blogs on his educational website www.effortfuleducator.com and follow him on Twitter @effortfuleduktr.

Brain dumps

Brain dumps are simply a knowledge recall task. A 'brain dump' – a term coined by Agarwal, also known as blurting or 'knowledge drops' – simply refers to dumping as much information from the brain about a specific topic or unit (long-term memory, no notes) onto a piece of paper. This is a classic example of a **low effort, high impact** task for students to complete. This can be a 'do now' task to begin a lesson where the teacher will give the students an allotted amount of time to recall as much as they can from memory about a specific event, individual, concept, theory and so on. Although, as mentioned in the previous chapter, younger students may struggle with this type of task.

I prefer to ask students to do this on their own rather than in pairs or groups (although this type of task can be completed with others) as the retrieval practice will be more effective individually. Whilst there are many benefits to students working together, we are aware of the potential problems of some students retrieving more or all of the information on behalf of the group. Nonetheless, there are ways to tackle this by instructing that each individual must contribute to the brain dump (either verbally or through written answers) and if there is some retrieval struggle the students can support one another.

You could simply ask students to complete a brain dump in their books, on a post-it note or mini whiteboards (depending how much content you want students to retrieve and if you wish to refer to it at a later point or not). You could provide prompts with headings to provide clarity about which specific areas or units you want students to focus on, but be careful not to provide too much information, as it will make the retrieval easier. There are lots of variations of the brain dump-style task in this book. Similar to brain dumps are picture prompts. I show a picture to the class – that could be a photo, illustration, map, portrait or diagram – and then ask students to recall information linked to that image. Obviously, the image itself does provide retrieval support but the key is to ensure that students recall relevant information, not describe what they can see. That could be a separate task in itself but it is *not* retrieval practice.

Picture prompt

Task: Explain how each image is connected to Henry VIII and the break with Rome. Explain in your own words, from memory.

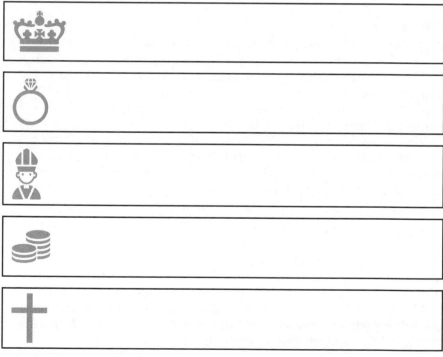

Figure 2 Picture prompt: King Henry VIII

For example, if I started the lesson with a photo of a World War One soldier with trench foot (a common disease and problem that occurred as a result of cold, wet and damp living conditions in the trenches) then students could – either verbally or through writing – retrieve what they known about trench foot. This could include why the disease was common, the side effects, how it was treated and so on. This information won't be provided from the image it comes from their subject knowledge and from prior learning. However, if students were to simply describe the condition of trench foot with swelling and its visual appearance then this is simply providing a description. A good way to ensure retrieval and not description takes place is through explicit modelling of an example to the class to make the difference clear. If you do use this technique already or will intend to then I can highly recommend visiting the pixabay website, which contains a huge library of over a million high-quality images that are available to use, without any copyright or attribution requirements (royalty free). It is such a great website.

Quiz, Quiz, Trade

This is a Kagan approach to learning. The Kagan approach involves promoting cooperation and communication with the focus on engaging every learner. Whilst those are all very important aspects of every classroom, Kagan approaches can be considered as dismissive of a traditional classroom. It is important to remember the work of Professor Rob Coe (*et al*, 2014) where he highlighted that engagement can be a poor proxy for learning – just because students are engaged does not mean they are actually learning.[1] We must embrace engagement in the classroom but not at the cost of learning. 'Quiz, Quiz, Trade' is a Kagan game that I believe successfully promotes communication, engagement *and* retrieval practice.

This game involves students both asking questions and answering them with one another in the classroom. The teacher can create the cards with a question on one side and the answer on the back. This will involve some cutting (which I do try to avoid, but no gluing so that's good!). Alternatively, depending on your class, the students can write the questions and answers based on content studied. However, it may be worth the teacher quickly scanning to check that the students have written the correct answers or that the level of challenge is appropriate, as this can be difficult for some students to grasp when creating their own questions, ranging from the obviously easy to ridiculously difficult!

---

1. Core, R., Aloisi, C., Higgins, S. and Major, L. E. (2014) *What makes great teaching? Review of the underpinning research.* Retrieved from: www.bit.ly/2x0NoR6

You can download a blank template; use post-it notes or even double-sided mini whiteboards. This is another relatively low effort and easy to create task. The questions can be content-based or focus on vocabulary with definitions on the back. This activity works very well with modern foreign languages, in addition to all other subjects focusing on subject-specific terminology.

Each student will have a piece of card or paper with a question on one side and the answer on the other. A student will ask the other the question that is on their card – this is the first quiz question. The student being asked has to try to answer and their partner will inform them if they are correct or not. Then the testee – the student that has just answered the first question – becomes the questioner, asking the second question to their peer as the roles are reversed. Once both students have answered each other's questions they trade cards and then ask that question to a different student with the process being repeated, hence 'Quiz, Quiz, Trade'.

Quiz, Quiz, Trade can be used at the start of a lesson to retrieve previous material or at the end of a lesson to check understanding of the content that has been taught in the lesson. It can also be used as an interactive style revision game with students asking and answering questions amongst each other, working well at both primary and secondary level.

Question:	Answer:
Question:	Answer:
Question:	Answer:
Question:	Answer:
Question:	Answer:
Question:	Answer:

Figure 3 Quiz, Quiz, Trade

Cops and Robbers

This task is similar to Quiz, Quiz, Trade as it combines retrieval practice with communication skills, working with others. Another very simple strategy.

The 'cops' column is for students to write as much as they can from memory about a specific topic, or previously-covered material in a set amount of time – similar to a brain dump. Once the students have had about four to five minutes to write as much as they can from memory they then have to complete the 'robbers' section. This is where everyone in the class needs to get out of their seats and read their peers work, swapping and sharing their ideas and content. Students will often read another student's 'cop column' and see information that they forgot or didn't have time to include. When this happens they should add that extra information to the 'rob column'. It is not designed as a competition but instead focus on recall and working with others.

Your own knowledge and recall...

Information you have 'stolen' from your peers...

Figure 4 Cops and Robbers

After sharing this idea in my first book *Love to Teach*, history teacher Emily Folorunsho adapted this idea for her younger students by providing some support through headings, as shown in figure 5. The idea remains the same with retrieval and then seeking information from peers but this provides more specific focus and structure.

Factor	Your own knowledge and recall... 	 Information you have 'stolen' from your peers...
Victorian London		
Working conditions		
Living conditions		
Jack the Ripper		
Other key facts...		

Figure 5 Cops and Robbers by Emily Folorunsho

Walkabout Bingo

Walkabout Bingo continues to be one of my favourite classroom tasks. I like it because it involves retrieval practice and it encourages students to talk to one another (going beyond the typical think, pair and share, as they have to engage with different members of the class). It is very simple to create and also very adaptable, as I have used it with all age groups and across different subjects and topics.

Q. What is the name of a person accused of committing heresy? A: Heretic Name: Abby	Q. Describe the crime of treason. A: Plotting against monarchy Name: Katie	Q. Name an item that was smuggled in the 17th & 18th century? A: Brandy, Silk Name: Sophie
Q. Give a cause of crime. A: Poverty Name: Beth	Q. State one reason highway robbery increased. A: Cheap guns Name: Owen	Q. State one reason highway robbery declined. A: Banks Name: David
Q. Who was the fictitious leader of the Luddites? A: Ned Ludd Name: John	Q. What did the Luddites damage? A: Textile machinery Name: Charlotte	Q. What was the name of the riot that happened in South Wales and saw men dressed as women? A: Rebecca Riots Name: Megan
Q. Describe living conditions in the 18th & 19th century. A: Awful Name: Robert	Q. Name a crime associated with technology. A: Hacking Name: Courtney	Q. Give an example of terrorism. A: 911 Name: Chloe
Q. Name a crime associated with motoring. A: Speeding Name: Miss K Jones	Q. Give a cause of crime from both the Tudor period and 20th century. A: Poverty Name: Graham	Q. How has technology helped prevent or solve crime. A: DNA Name: Adam

Figure 6 Walkabout Bingo: Crime and punishment

The concept of the activity is that students will be given a sheet with different questions linked to the topic or subject, as shown in figure 6. They cannot answer those questions themselves. Students need to ask their peers each of the questions. They can only ask someone a question once, encouraging everyone to interact and get involved.

The aim of the game is to have all questions answered by different members of the class and the first person to do so will shout 'bingo', bringing the game to an end. Then time is given to go through the answers. This task also allows an opportunity to include questions from further back, encouraging interleaving and spaced practice. It is an engaging activity that focuses on retrieval and communication. The teacher can decide how long to spend on this activity by the amount of questions included. I also think I enjoy Walkabout Bingo because I like to walk around the class and listen to students asking and answering questions with one another, just like Quiz, Quiz, Trade and Cops and Robbers. I sometimes play along with this game too, so students can ask me questions. I have noticed that the questions they ask me tend to be the most challenging, illustrating which questions are proving the most difficult for the class to answer. This is a good example of verbal retrieval practice in action.

Retrieval relay race

This is another activity that also involves retrieval practice and working with others. This task is designed to promote retrieval but also stretch and challenge students to remember as much information as they can with no repetition of information.

For each retrieval relay race there will be a key topic, event, individual or idea. There will be four boxes, representing each member of the relay team. In the first box the student will write as much as they can recall about the specified topics, for this example it was Henry VIII. Once they have completed their first box they will need to find three other members of the class to fill in the rest of the boxes, retrieving information about Henry VIII. They cannot repeat any material in the boxes or they will be disqualified, so this task requires the students to read the filled in box/boxes in order to retrieve different information. Once the second box has been filled with different information, the third box will be filled in by another student. Whilst students are filling in their relay box they can be doing the same for another student (so no one is waiting around with nothing to do). As no information can be repeated that is any other box it, therefore, becomes more challenging.

Retrieval relay race: Fill in the first box with as much information as you can about our topic. Then you must ask someone else to complete the second box – remember they cannot repeat information already in the first box! Do the same for boxes three and four.

Henry VIII

Henry VIII was the second Tudor King, son of Henry VII. He is the most famous for having six wives – divorced, beheaded, died, divorced, beheaded and survived. He is remembered for his larger appearance, lavish spending and making many changes in England. He had three children – Mary, Elizabeth and Edward – but despite having two daughters, it was a son he was desperate for.

Henry VIII

Henry was not originally the main heir to the throne, he had an older brother Arthur but he died so Henry became King once his father died in 1509. Henry married Catherine of Aragon from Spain, she was married to his brother Arthur before he died. Catherine gave birth to Mary but she could not give birth to a son so Henry divorced her, but it wasn't easy to get a divorce from her back then.

Henry VIII

Henry closed down the monasteries in England and Wales. He closed them to gain more money and because he broke with Rome and wanted his people to obey him and be loyal to him not the Pope. Henry died knowing he would pass his throne to his son Edward, but he didn't know that all of his three children would rule but none of them would have their own child and heir!

Henry VIII

When Henry fell out with the Pope, because the Pope wouldn't let him divorce his wife, he then created the Church of England. This was different to the Catholic Church and Henry made himself the Head of the Church so that he could do what he wanted and have his divorce! This also made Henry a lot of money too, as well as even more powerful than before.

Figure 7 Retrieval relay race: History

For the final box, a different student will have to read all three boxes and try to recall more information about Henry VIII that has not yet been included. I have been surprised many times at the information students are able to recall, the fourth box always challenges students to go far beyond the six wives narrative in this example!

My students have found this to be an enjoyable task and it consolidates knowledge in addition to providing a free recall opportunity for everyone in the class. You could change how many boxes are used it can be four or make it even harder with six but I think four is ideal because you have to factor in the time it takes students to read each of the boxes before they recall and write. A time limit is also optional. I use this as a classroom resource but it can also be used as a revision activity too.

Although I haven't used this resource digitally, it does have the potential to become an online document if your school uses devices and has access to collaborative tools such as Google Docs. A lot of the resources, other than the online quizzing tools, are carried out in books or on worksheet templates as I am an advocate for providing learners with lots of writing opportunities in the lesson and I am very aware and mindful of screen time. There are lots of benefits when it comes to technology enhancing teaching and learning in addition to supporting teacher workload, which I explore in more depth in this chapter. I would be keen to see if or how any teachers have adapted the resources from this book to a digital format.

List it!

Another simple free recall task. This involves asking students to list as much as they can in an allotted amount of time. Possible suggestions for listing:

- List as many keywords as you can connected to our topic.
- List as many key facts as you can linked to our topic.
- List as many key facts as you can about a previous topic (spaced practice).
- List as many key events or individuals we have studied.
- List as many causes of X as you can.
- List as many consequences of Y as you can.
- List as many themes as you can.

Once students have listed as many factors as they can you could also ask them to swap and share their lists with their peers and to include any other facts or pieces of information they have not included but their peers have, similar to the Cops and Robbers. The first example was completed by a Year 9 student at the beginning of a lesson, studying the causes of World War One.

Causes	Individuals	Keywords
• The alliance system with the Triple Entente and Triple Alliances.	• Franz Ferdinand	• Alliances
	• Gavrilo Princip	• Militarism
• The murder of Archduke Franz Ferdinand.	• Kaiser Wilhelm	• Imperialism
	• Tsar Nicholas	• Nationalism
• Countries were competing to have the biggest armies and navies and in order to prove theirs was the best, they wanted to go to war and win.		• Empire
		• Colonialism
		• Assassination
		• Propaganda
• There were lots of countries jealous of the British empire of that scale themselves too!		• Central powers
		• Dreadnought

Figure 8 List it! History

The second example on the following page is from a Welsh second language lesson recalling key vocabulary linked to different topics studied. This combines retrieval practice with spaced practice and interleaving (explained in more depth in the next chapter) and as we can see this identifies areas of strong recall and areas of struggle.

If you want your classes to retrieve deeper and precise subject knowledge (rather than a general overview of a unit or period) and recall a specific topic the list it category can be adapted to do so. Instead of asking students to retrieve information about the causes of World War One the task could be adapted to selecting one cause, for example the alliance system, and students have to list as many points and key facts as they can linked to the alliances. I like the flexibility of this task when it comes to thinking about what information you want your students to be able to retrieve.

Ysgol (School)	Bwyd (Foods)	Hobiau (Hobbies)
• Hanes	• Afal	• Rygbi
• Mathemateg	• Siocled	• Pel droed
• Saesneg	• Te	• Rhedeg
• Cymraeg	• Coffi	• Nofio
• Gwyddoniaeth	• Bara	• Dawnsio
• Athro	• Cawl	
• Gwaith dosbarth	• Moron	
• Llyfrau	• Bisgedi	
• Wisg ysgol	• Crempog	
• Amser cinio	• Sglodion	
• Addysg Grefyddol	• FFa pob	
• Miwsig	• Hufen ia	
• Celf	• Pys	
• Technoleg	• Reis	

Figure 9 List it! Welsh language

Throwback Thursday or Flashback Friday

As an end of lesson task on a Thursday or Friday (or any day of the week for that matter) ask students to create a series of ten questions based on the lesson content, either from that lesson or week, and they should include the answers too. Students will then return to those questions a week later, or longer, to see what they can remember and recall. Students could answer their own questions or be given questions created by one of their peers to answer, this depends on the individuals in your class, as you will know which will work best.

This can easily become part of a regular routine and, by doing so over the term and academic year, students will collect a bank of questions and answers to test themselves at a later date for revision. A great way to do this is to write the questions on the left side of a sheet of A4 paper with answers on the right. Once all ten questions and answers are filled in students then fold over the answer page so the following week they will just see the side with the questions but on completion can open up the folded quiz to reveal the answers to self check and correct their questions.

Self-testing to promote independent retrieval practice

Self-testing is really important because there will be many times, as part of home-learning, when revising or during higher education when students will not have the support of their teacher. They will need to know how to independently revise and check their knowledge and understanding of topics.

Rebecca Foster, head of English, author and TES podcast host has reflected on how well self-testing has worked within the English department at her school. Foster wrote, 'One of the best things we've done this year is introduce self-quizzing', this was an idea Foster adapted from Joe Kirby taken from the book *Battle Hymn of the Tiger Teachers: The Michaela Way*. Foster commented that: 'Not only does retrieval practice homework complement our approach to homework (activities which have value but require no marking), but we have also seen students' knowledge improve as well as their confidence.' It is so useful when teachers and departments trial new strategies then feedback and reflect sharing this with other educators – whether they worked or not, but this example focuses on sharing an idea that worked well.

To achieve this with self-testing, Foster and her colleagues in the English department provided all students across Key Stages 3 and 4 with knowledge organisers (KO) for the texts being studied. The KO included information that all students were required and expected to know. Foster writes that 'the information on the KO is that which we want all students to be able to recall with ease, which will free up working memory when they are tackling challenging skills such as writing an essay on a text'.

All students were given an exercise book with the specific aim to use them purely for self-quizzing homework and everyone is expected to spend a minimum of 30 minutes every week self-quizzing on their KO. Teachers can easily check that this has been carried out as students efforts and progress are instantly visible in their self-quizzing books.

It is very important to add that Foster explicitly modelled self-testing when introducing this concept to her students. Foster explains how she did this: 'I turned my copy of the KO over and then wrote down as much as I could. I then flipped the KO back over and checked the accuracy of what I had written down.' In addition to this Foster self-corrected any errors and filled in any gaps.

This is a brilliant reflection of how independent retrieval practice can work outside of the classroom. To see examples of this strategy in action and read more by Foster visit www.thelearningprofession.com and I suggest you follow Rebecca Foster on Twitter (if you aren't already) @TLPMrsL.

Don't underestimate the mini whiteboard

Mini whiteboards are great and can be used as part of a regular 'do now' starter routine to practice retrieval. They can ensure that all learners are participating and involved in the retrieval practice. If students do not answer or respond then this is made visibly clear for the teacher to be aware of and act on just through a quick glance and scan of the room. The teacher can easily see if everyone in the class is listening, following instructions, understanding and engaging in retrieval practice by using the mini whiteboards.

Strategies that focus on hands up and volunteering verbal answers tend to appeal to more confident and vocal students whereas mini whiteboards can be a good method for the quieter or reluctant students in your class. Mini whiteboards can assist students with building their confidence and encouraging them to participate more in class discussions. The fact that answers can be easily wiped off and removed also contributes to the low and no stakes element of retrieval practice. It is very rare that a teacher will collect and record answers from mini whiteboards so they aren't associated with testing or being high stakes in the classroom. The teacher is able to provide immediate and instant feedback by responding to answers on mini whiteboards. Mini whiteboards do not require any marking as the feedback is live in the lesson, consequently having a positive impact on teacher workload.

Sherrington has described mini whiteboards as his number one bit of classroom kit. Sherrington blogged about mini whiteboards, writing: 'The trick is to use them really well. You need to drill the class to use them seriously, to do the "show me" action simultaneously in a crisp, prompt manner and, crucially, you need to get students to hold up the boards long enough for you to engage with their responses. Who is stuck? Who has got it right? Are there any interesting variations/ideas? Use the opportunity to ask, "why did you say that? How did you know that?", and so on. It takes practice to make this technique work but it's so good when done well.'[2]

---

2. Sherrington, T. (2017) 'Ten teaching techniques to practise – deliberately', *Teacherhead* [Online] 25 April. Retrieved from: www.bit.ly/2nWWvR3

If your students have access to technology and devices such as tablets, you can use the screen as a digital mini whiteboard. This removes the issue of pens and whiteboard erasers but has all the benefits of a regular mini whiteboard!

Retrieval grids

There are lots of versions of retrieval grids and my most downloaded resource is the retrieval practice challenge grid that is featured in Chapter 4, as a revision resource. The retrieval grid on the following page is slightly different but it does combine retrieval and spaced practice.

This grid can contain as many boxes as you deem suitable. The amount of boxes equate to the amount of lessons the grid will be used for. I had three lessons a week with my GCSE classes so six boxes were used for two weeks of lessons, nine boxes being three weeks, and so on. I have used this with upper school classes, although this can be used and adapted for younger students too.

The idea behind this type of grid/activity is very simple. Each box will contain a specific element of a topic already studied – no new material. The box could refer to a concept, event, individual, key term or date. At the start of a lesson every student will pick one of the boxes and write as much as they know from memory about that chosen category (similar to a brain dump). The following lesson the same grid will be on display (or printed if you chose to do so) and students have to pick a different category to recall as much information as they can. Students cannot repeat a box, every lesson a new box containing a different factor must be selected and be the focus of the recall. Eventually, all students will have retrieved information about every factor in the grid.

Retrieval grids: Each lesson you must select an individual and write down as much as you can remember from memory about that individual focusing on their significance and contribution. You cannot refer to a box more than once.

Figure 10 A retrieval grid

Throughout the process this task identified gaps in students knowledge for them to act on before the next lesson. Apart from the initial lesson, the students will know what they will need to retrieve next lesson and they may decide in advance which factor they wish to focus on for the upcoming lesson.

A student once asked me if this activity encouraged cheating because they knew what they would have to write about next lesson based on the boxes they hadn't addressed so far. I explained that this didn't encourage cheating as this task was identifying gaps in their knowledge or areas where they were lacking in confidence. The fact that they were deciding to act on that in advance to be prepared in the lesson is brilliant and exactly what they should be doing, a clear use of initiative and independent learning, thus illustrating one of the indirect benefits of testing as discussed in the previous chapter.

This again links to Sherrington's point about specifying the knowledge, it can be argued that reducing the element of surprise reduces the level of challenge but I wasn't telling the class what areas or topics they had to focus on, they identified this themselves by viewing the grid and deciding which topics they wanted to write about because they felt confident and knowledgeable in comparison to the other boxes.

A student told me that they had left Galen until the final lesson using this grid because this was a specific individual where they felt they only possessed basic and limited knowledge and understanding, recognising they often struggled to recall the significance and contribution made by Galen. This led to a discussion to clear up some confusion and as the student knew they would have to recall information about Galen the following lesson without any support, as it was the only box left, this gave them the nudge to revisit their notes, self-test and prepare for the retrieval in upcoming the lesson.

To create this grid I referred back to the specification and ensured the boxes contained headings based on essential content and material for this unit. This grid included an overview of factors that students must know (in this case it was individuals connected to the development of health and medicine), be able to recall and use in the context of a history answer. In the lesson I would give my students five minutes to recall what they could about the box they had chosen then I would give them a few more minutes to then check that information against their notes, self-correcting, ticking or allowing them to add more information in another colour that they hadn't originally included.

This activity was good because, over that period of time, students built up a collated set of retrieval notes that covered a unit and, by doing so, it had motivated students to fill the gaps in the knowledge as well as providing plenty of opportunities for regular retrieval. This task also ensured retrieval became part of our classroom routine as the grid was projected on the board when students entered and they would immediately select a box from the grid and use the time wisely to recall as much as they could about that individual. It is a very simple, adaptable and flexible retrieval resource.

I would advise against using an A4 grid as that limits the amount a student can write and recall. In my experience an A3 grid worked better or not actually writing on a grid at all but instead using the grid headings and retrieving notes onto lined paper or books so they were able to retrieve as much information as they could in the allocated time – the problem with a template can be that if a student fills a box with writing then they stop but potentially they could challenge themselves to recall more information (also unnecessary photocopying/printing too).

Challenge grid

Wiliam wrote that 'if you make learning too easy, students don't have to work hard to make sense of what they are learning, and as a result will forget it quickly',[3] but if we make learning too difficult students can also become frustrated and stop working.[4] As teachers we need to ensure that the difficulties we present our students are accessible and desirable. Desirable difficulties have already been mentioned briefly, but credit should be given to researchers Elizabeth and Robert Bjork as they termed this phrase that is widely used in education today. Desirable difficulties refer to the level of challenge that requires encoding and retrieval to support learning, comprehension and remembering. This is desirable in the classroom.

If we consider an interactive game – on an Xbox or PlayStation for example – game designers create a game with the intention of it gradually becoming harder and, ultimately, desirable difficulties apply with gaming. If a game is too easy, players can easily get bored and move onto something more challenging and gripping. In the same sense, if a game is too difficult this will frustrate and even anger the player to the point where they give up and resort to another game where they are more likely to achieve success. The first few levels are always designed to be relatively easy, providing the player with a sense of achievement and a confidence boost. The player understands that the game will become increasingly challenging as they progress through the game, and thus become even more rewarding, emphasising once again a desirable difficulty must be something people can overcome through increased effort.[5]

A challenge grid is a resource that has been widely used teachers to promote challenge and retrieval practice in the classroom. It is simply a grid with a range of questions for students to generate an answer (the amount of boxes with questions can vary you can decide). The aim of the challenge grid is to provide different questions that vary in the level of difficulty they pose. This resource works well if you have a mixed ability class, as there are questions that everyone should be able to

---

3. Wiliam, D. (2016) 'The 9 things every teacher should know', *TES* [Online] 2 September. Retrieved from: www.bit.ly/33I1nJ4

4. Smith, M. and Firth, J. (2018) *Psychology in the Classroom: A Teacher's Guide to What Works*. Abingdon, Oxon: Routledge, p. 68.

5. Bjork, E. and Bjork, R. (2011) 'Making things hard on yourself, but in a good way: Creating desirable difficulties to enhance learning', *Psychology and the Real World: Essays Illustrating Fundamental Contributions to Society*, pp. 55–64.

access. The challenge grids are designed to challenge every individual in the classroom. The challenge is focused on the subject content, not the activity itself, and only requires a very brief explanation in regards to instruction. Each question will be worth a certain amount of points and the points increase as the level of difficulty increases, as a video game or most quizzes would. I usually allow students about eight to ten minutes to answer as many questions as they can using the retrieval practice strategy from memory – not using any notes or their books – and they can select which questions they want to answer. Depending on the length or type of answers you could provide the answers on the next slide or a separate sheet of paper for students to self-check and correct. Alternatively, you could discuss the answers as a class depending on how much time you wish to dedicate to this activity.

I tend to use the challenge grid at the beginning of a lesson but I have also used it as a revision activity too. The example in figure 11 was for a Year 6 social studies class in Abu Dhabi, in preparation for upcoming annual National Day celebrations. You may or may not be able to tell but the level of difficulty increases as the amount of points increases in a similar approach to gaming. There is another version of a challenge grid that has a specific focus on vocabulary as shown in figure 12 where students had to provide definitions in their own words or write about that key term in the context of our topic.

What day is National Day celebrated?	Describe traditional dress worn on National Day.	Who was the founding leader of the UAE?	Which emirate is the largest emirate in the UAE?
How many years will the UAE be celebrating this year?	List the seven emirates in the UAE.	What is the name of the UAE national bird?	What is the name of the UAE national anthem?
List three ways people celebrate National Day in the UAE.	What year did the UAE form the joint Nation Agreement?	What is the name of the largest Mosque in the UAE?	List three dishes eaten during National Day celebrations.

1 point   2 points   3 points   4 points

Figure 11 National Day challenge grid

1. Democracy	4. Apathy	7. Pressure group	10. Interest group
2. Direct democracy	5. Referendum	8. Franchise	11. Devolution
3. Representative democracy	6. Turnout	9. Suffragette	12. Insider groups
1 point	2 points	3 points	4 points

Figure 12 Vocabulary challenge grid

Case study: Retrieval practice and what it looks like in a classroom

This year on Twitter I have been keeping up to date with the tweets and blogs from Tom Johns who is Associate Assistant Headteacher and a science teacher at Kingsmead School, Somerset. Retrieval practice is something Tom has discussed a lot online therefore I was keen to have Tom feature in this book and this is what he had to share about his classroom experience and professional learning journey.

2018 marked my tenth year in teaching. If I was a footballer this may have ended in a testimonial, it didn't, but it did start with an epiphany.

The previous year I attended and presented at a TeachMeet event in Devon. The keynote speakers at the event were Dr Yana Weinstein and Dr Megan Sumeracki. They told delegates all about their 'Six strategies for effective learning', the two ideas that struck a chord the most were retrieval practice and dual coding. It took the following 12 months of research, review and reflection to embed these ideas into my day-to-day teaching. It has now become second nature.

Since my NQT year I have been saying to students: 'To be a successful scientist you need to think of science as one, not three, separate sciences (biology, chemistry and physics), to do this you need to link the ideas together.' For many years I thought this was an easy request to make of students. How hard could it be? I was wrong – I know this now. One should never assume and that is exactly what I did, I assumed students could do this. This is the difference between explicit and implicit instruction. Supporting students is my bread and butter, but it needed the kick-start that Weinstein and Sumeracki gave me to start my paradigm shift. Instead of asking students to learn, I now tell them to learn. So now instead of asking the students to link the core ideas together from biology, chemistry and physics, I tell them how to do it. In the run up to the GCSE exams, there is often an issue of students leaving their revision too late, let alone not knowing how to revise at all and I have focused on developing this.

At the start of each new topic I give students a checklist. This checklist is made up of numbered statements linked to the topic specification. When we start a new lesson, along with the title, I ask students to find the number of the lesson on the checklist. This gives the lesson meaning and also means the students can tick off when they have mastered sections. It also becomes very useful when students are absent as they can quickly compare their checklists to other students' to see their 'missing' sections and, of course, aid their retrieval.

One of my missions is to make home learning meaningful and cut down on my own workload. I do not set 'research'-based home learning any longer but past paper questions at Key Stage 4. These are not also linked to the topic the students are currently studying but is often interleaved. The home learning question sheets have a cut down version of the topic checklists which are embedded after the questions. These cover just the areas on the checklist that the home learning is testing. The home learning is then peer/ self marked, and I just take in and record the scores. Poorly answered home learning can then be used again later for further retrieval work. I put all these home learning sheets in a folder which students then get back in Year 11 to act as a revision guide.

From the start of the first day back in the second term I give Year 11 students a question a day retrieval revision sheet. These questions cover all areas of the specification and use the ideas of retrieval and spaced practice, as well as interleaving. The questions use the premise of a little and often. I get students to highlight questions they are happy with in green and those they had to look up to highlight in orange so they can go back to them at a later date. Every couple of weeks I use some of the questions students should have looked at as retrieval starter questions in the labs and also provide copies to give to parents. Involving parents in retrieval practice is important.

At the end of topics I provide students with an A to Z sheet in which they have to find keywords and themes in the topic starting with the letters A to Z. Students can create their own retrieval sheets from their A to Z. On the reverse students are asked to draw a diagram of some form to represent their words. I have found encouraging dual coding also benefits long-term retrieval.

You can find more examples and resources for the classroom on his wonderful blog www.sciencetltoolkit.wordpress.com and you can follow Tom on Twitter @TJohns85.

Retrieval practice and technology: The TPACCK model

My adaptation of the well-known TPACK model, which I referred to as the TPACCK model, first featuring in *Love to Teach*, builds on the work of Lee Shulman, Punya Mishra and Matthew Koehler. Their writing and research ranging from the 1980s to 2019. Shulman created the original PCK model where he stressed the importance of 'both content and pedagogical knowledge' for teachers.[6] The TPACK model by Mishra and Koehler focused on the combination of 'technological, pedagogical and content knowledge'. The model explains how a teacher can use their experience and knowledge of effective teaching methods to consider how to incorporate the technology into these methods. If the teacher lacks the knowledge and understanding of how the technology works, then this will cause problems and end up being a barrier to learning. In the same way, if a teacher knows how to use technology and has a good comprehension of teaching and learning approaches but has limited knowledge of the subject content then this can also have a negative impact on learning. Knowing subject material but having a lack of knowledge on how to communicate that information through pedagogy will also be unsuccessful. When using technology all aspects are very important and need to complement one another. If a teacher has deep subject knowledge, is able to use effective pedagogical strategies combined with a good understanding of the technology being used, then all of this can lead to greater success in the classroom.

In September 2018 the TPACK model received an upgrade, known as TPACKx, by Mishra and this version included a focus on contextual knowledge and factors. Mishra writes 'contextual knowledge would be everything from a teacher's awareness of the kind of technologies available for them and their students; to their knowledge of the school, district and state policies that they have to function within'.[7] This is clearly all encompassing, taking into consideration a wide range of factors teachers have to consider and be aware of when integrating technology successfully into the classroom, some that are out of the control of the teacher or leader.

6. Shulman, L. S. (1986) 'Those Who Understand: Knowledge Growth in Teaching', *Educational Researcher* 15 (2) pp. 4–14.
7. Mishra, P. (2018) 'The TPACK diagram gets an upgrade', *Punya Mishra's Web* [Online] 10 September. Retrieved from: www.bit.ly/35SaTuT

TPACCK: Technological, Pedagogical, Cognitive and Content Knowledge

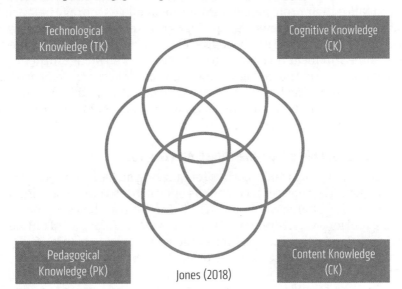

Figure 13 The TPACCK model

I added another 'C' to the model to focus on cognitive knowledge, essentially the science of learning. As educators we should combine our content and pedagogical knowledge with our understanding of cognitive psychology when using technology too. Here are the main components of the TPACCK model:

- Using quizzing as a method to support learning is a pedagogical strategy and demonstrates our understanding of cognitive psychology and the benefits of retrieval practice.

- To create a challenging and appropriate online quiz for students to complete requires subject knowledge from the teacher. We are using technology efficiently to create, deliver and record quizzes. Without the subject knowledge we would be unable to write questions that cover a wide breadth and depth of content.

- Without pedagogical knowledge we would not consider effective techniques such as quizzing. Being unaware of the impact of retrieval practice for supporting learning would mean that we only use quizzing as an assessment tool instead of a learning tool.

The TPACCK model has now also been used by teachers and schools as a way to tailor their professional development and encourage balance, ensuring that subject knowledge, pedagogical knowledge, technological knowledge and cognitive knowledge are not neglected. I read a range of books, some will focus on developing my subject knowledge, other books can be more generic and pedagogy focused, and others are dedicated to cognitive science or technology in the classroom. These factors shouldn't be considered separate to one another, but instead combined to achieve success and impact in the classroom.

Quizizz: The best online multiple-choice quizzing tool

There are so many apps and websites for quizzing inside and outside of the classroom. The choice is tremendous but it can also be overwhelming. **Quizizz** is – in my humble opinion – the best multiple-choice online quizzing tool for a variety of reasons. There are lots of wonderful online quizzing tools and apps but I wanted to focus on Quizziz because of the range of unique features it has to offer. It is continually growing in popularity with both teachers and students alike. I have always stressed that technology should be used to impact teaching and learning and/or support teacher workload, both factors are incredibly important. I believe Quizizz can support and enhance retrieval practice with many features to support teacher workload too. The same approach applies with edtech (technology in the classroom), **low effort, high impact**.

Here are the main reasons why I think Quizizz is brilliant for retrieval practice in the classroom and what makes this quizzing tool stand out:

- As Quizizz can be accessed through a browser it can therefore be accessed on any device with internet. Regardless of what brand of technology your school uses everyone can use Quizizz, which comes with no built in charges either as it is totally free.

- It is very easy for both teachers and students to use. When it comes to technology simplicity is key.

- Unlike other quizzing tools, with Quizizz there is no need to input class lists as the students can do this themselves. If they decide to input a silly or offensive name, then the teacher has the option to remove that immediately too.

- Although retrieval practice is intended to be low stakes, that doesn't mean we can't analyse results in our class to check and act on. Quizziz records and tracks the results for the teacher, no need for the teacher to record any data. Quizizz can break down information to show which questions the majority of the class answered correctly or incorrectly to gauge understanding at a class level, in addition to revealing a breakdown of individual students too.

- The teleport feature is genius. Quizizz allows the teacher to upload the quizzes they create to a public platform for other users (teachers or students) to access. Other online quizzes offer this feature and teachers can use another teachers quiz. The problem I found when looking at other quizzes online is that none of the quizzes were quite right for my classes and lessons – either the content was too easy, too difficult or included content not studied or relevant. The teleport feature allows the user to browse through other quizzes and select specific questions from others quizzes to teleport to their own quiz. So, for example, I may find a quiz where three of the questions are suitable but the rest of the quiz isn't appropriate so I can just teleport the three questions to my quiz. Once teleported I can even edit the multiple-choice answers too. This allows the teacher to create a personalised quiz for their classes in a fraction of the time! A simple yet great idea for the busy teacher. If a teacher has created a quiz then there is an option to email it to colleagues so that others in the department can use the same quiz with their classes, providing a great way of sharing practice and collaborating.

- The leaderboard feature is often a popular feature with many online quizzes but it causes me too much frustration. Sometimes – although not always as it depends on the class – my classes have used an online quizzing tool and the same students have dominated the leaderboard. This is not a surprise to the rest of the class or to myself, but it can have a demoralising effect on others. Competition can work in the classroom but it can also be a distraction or have a negative impact on the class, subsequently there is the option to keep or remove the leaderboard feature depending on your class and students.

- I really dislike that students are often rewarded for answering questions quickly. This encourages bad habits as later on we tell students to take time to read the questions carefully in exams. Removing the question timer stops students from rushing their answers but instead allows them to carefully read the question and consider their answer before selecting an option.

- The music playing in the background during a quiz can be annoying and distracting but again there is the option to remove it!

■ After every question answered a comical meme is revealed which students often like. The teacher can personalise this by creating their own memes, or they can remove it altogether.

■ Quizizz is continually adapting with new features for teachers and students, including the option to set quizzes as a homework. You can set a deadline that students must complete the quiz by. There is also a team option where students answer at their own pace but their results are grouped together by teams to create a sense of collaboration whilst still focusing on the retrieval aspect. Quizizz has introduced a test-style function, described on the site as 'a no-frills mode that is ideal for conducting a serious assessment', so Quizizz have the different options available. You can add audio clips, polls and maths equations to Quizizz quizzes too.

Plickers

This is another fantastic quizzing tool, especially if your school and students don't have access to technology as only one device is required – the teacher's device, who will scan the answers from the class. When using Plickers, you can use your own smartphone or tablet to do this. A teacher will need to set up an account on the website (www.plickers.com) and class lists need to be uploaded. Although this is much easier for teachers with one class or smaller class sizes – as inputting the class lists can be slightly time-consuming – once all the names are saved on the account, they can be used for the rest of the academic year.

The teacher can easily create their own multiple-choice quizzes on the website with a possibility of up to four multiple-choice answers or 'true'/'false'. The quizzes are then saved to use in the lesson. Students will each have their own card known as a paper clicker, which can be downloaded for free on the Plickers website. The cards are used by the students to answer questions. A question with a choice of answers will be projected onto the board and each student will hold their paper clicker card up to represent their answer. Everyone has a different card with a unique code so students cannot copy one another or see how others have answered because he or she must rotate the card to illustrate their answer. Plickers has been around a short while and I think it will continue to stand the test of time as a classroom quizzing tool.

Figure 14 Plickers in the classroom

Google Forms

At my school all students have their own Google Chromebook to use both inside and outside of lessons. Chromebooks have certainly not replaced written exercise books but instead teachers now have more options available to support and enhance teaching and learning. Google Forms has become a popular quizzing option at my school and is also used by lots of teachers around the world. You do not need access to a specific device to use Google Forms but you will need a Google account to create the quiz.

The main advantage of using Google Forms for retrieval practice is that it allows the teacher to create multiple-choice or free recall quizzes, thus providing opportunities for retrieval success and retrieval challenge. For the multiple-choice options you can set up a list of options or a multiple-choice grid and it can check answers too. For the free recall, students can write a short answer or a paragraph but this will require a teacher response and feedback. There is also the option to allow students to upload a file too. There are other features such as check boxes, the option to upload images or link to YouTube videos too. Therefore, it is a very versatile quizzing tool. It is also very user friendly and easy to navigate. There are ready-made classroom templates available from blank quizzes to exit tickets. Google Forms also records and tracks your data for you, even if you are using it as a low-stakes quiz it can still be used to gauge a class or individual results.

Case study: Using edtech for retrieval practice with Olly Lewis

Olly Lewis is Assistant Headteacher, responsible for teaching and learning at The British International School, Abu Dhabi. Olly is very passionate about technology in the classroom and I have learned a lot from him. Here he writes about how we can embrace technology in the classroom to support retrieval practice.

In recent years I've tried hard to ensure that when I use technology in the classroom it has a clear purpose, rather than being used simply as an engagement tool for the students. Since learning about the importance of retrieval practice and checking for understanding, I've realised that there are many edtech tools out there that fit the purpose of enhancing the learning experience, provide pathways for fast and effective feedback to student practice, reduce workload and ensure that technology supports my practice. I've always been a fan of getting students to elaborate on their learning and by vocalising their explanations, it gives me a clear picture of the mental model they've developed, where the gaps are and the specific content that needs clarifying.

Quizlet (www.quizlet.com) has been a well-known tool to aid learning for some years now and there are many facets to its expanding repertoire of exercises such as key terms lists as flash cards, mini tests, writing and speaking key phrases, battles, matching exercises and the Quizlet Live function. What's great about Quizlet is the fact that you, and your students, can mix it up in terms of how they are being asked to recall information, which prevents your recall strategies from being repetitive, it enables the teacher to really check that they've grasped a concept (and to which level of detail) and importantly prevents us from sticking to only one style of retrieval task, which can lead to students becoming unstuck in a high-stakes situation where they need to adjust. The fact that Quizlet enables us to vary the style of retrieval that we present the students with, despite the knowledge we are checking often remaining the same, leads to it standing the test of time.

Personally I enjoy using the Quizlet Live function the most, you can split the class up into random groups and students have to work collaboratively to correctly match key terms, definitions and images. This allows you time to wander the room and listen to the discussions the students are having around the subject matter, this richly informs me about where to go next and what to review. I find it akin to mini whiteboards, however in greater detail, as it's easier to see their thinking through the quality of their discussions as opposed to seeing only their final answer. The game emphasises collaboration over speed, promoting discussion amongst the students to ensure they select the correct response from the array of answers on their devices.

Mentimeter (www.menti.com) is another tool that enables us to engage our audience, receive instant feedback and check for understanding in our classroom without identifying specific students in a class. Often when students don't know an answer, or lack confidence, they will follow the crowd where possible but Mentimeter enables us to remove that barrier and take an active role in their learning. Giving students a voice is of huge importance and when we remove or reduce barriers and enable an honest response from students without being identified they will engage in the lessons, enhancing learning and providing the teacher with another opportunity to review content. I've found that Mentimeter is a first-rate tool that enables and promotes instant feedback from the audience in a low-stakes manner while enthusing students as they can see the results instantly.

Mentimeter has a multifaceted approach too, thanks to tools such as polls, quizzes, reflections, word clouds, opinion scales and more – all of which can be embedded into your presentations ready for use in lessons thanks to their handy templates. These functions provide ample opportunity to survey the class, promote self-reflection and delve deeper into learning once again purposefully using technology to support the teachers checking for understanding while enhancing the learning of the students.

You can follow Olly on Twitter @OLewis_coaching and visit his blog www.ollylewislearning.com

Snakes and Ladders

A classic game that can be easily adapted for the classroom. Thanks to teacher and leader Pete Sanderson for originally creating and sharing this 'Snakes and Ladders' template for free. Print the template (and ask the maths department if they will loan you some dice, if you don't already have some) and then students can play this popular game whilst retrieving information from previous lessons.

Originally, Pete created the Snakes and Ladders template with a focus on Bloom's taxonomy, which you can see in figure 15. I have adapted it in my lessons by adjusting the questions to focus on retrieval and spaced practice. As the game progresses the level of challenge can increase with questions focusing on content studied further back as the player moves forwards. The start of the game will include questions from recently covered material and the end of the game will include questions based on lesson content from weeks ago or further.

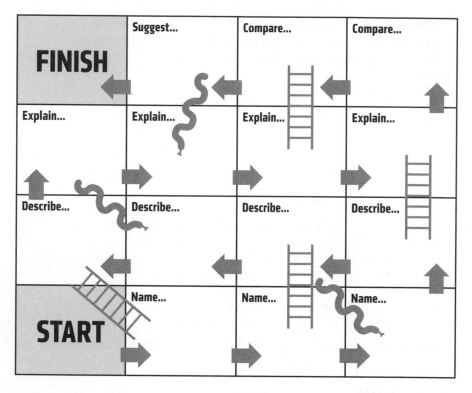

Figure 15 Snakes and Ladders template

In regards to answers I usually allow students to play the game for about eight to ten minutes as I walk around listening to their answers and conversations, then I will bring the class together to discuss and go over answers and I am able to say, 'Emily your answer and points about imperialism were very good can you share that with the rest of the class?'. Although it may seem I have put Emily on the spot because she didn't volunteer, I have already praised her and said her answer was correct to give her the confidence to share this knowledge with her peers.

You could even give students a blank template and ask them to create their own retrieval practice Snakes and Ladders game that can be played during another lesson.

Retrieval Roulette by Adam Boxer

Retrieval Roulette had been well-received and proven popular online, especially amongst science teachers, but it has also been adapted across a wide range of subjects due to its simplicity and effectiveness. This task is a classic example of embedding regular retrieval in the classroom.

It's creator, Adam Boxer, has reflected that knowing the potential that retrieval practice has for supporting student learning, he was keen to implement a simple, powerful routine for encouraging regular retrieval with his science classes. For each topic, Boxer creates a set of 'flash cards' of key ideas in question and answer form. The cards are focused to only include the material necessary and nothing extraneous. Boxer will print off a set with all the questions and answers and give it to students at the beginning of a unit and inform learners that all of his upcoming verbal questions will be based on these flash cards. They are expected to begin learning them off by heart and referring to them in both their verbal and written answers.

Boxer uses this activity regularly in his lessons, ensuring that his classes receive a mini-quiz using the contents of the flash cards he provided previously. To do this he uses an Excel programme, which he has aptly named 'Retrieval Roulette', to randomly select questions from the full set contained in the spreadsheet and then display the questions on the board for the students in his class.

The quiz will contain five questions from any point in the course, again linking spaced and retrieval practice in addition to including five questions from a current topic. Boxer will give students ten minutes to answer in the back of their books, so he is able to view their responses later if he chooses to do so and students can peer-assess answers. Boxer will then ask his class to raise their hands if they got question one right, then question two and so on. Based on their responses, Boxer will pick a question that many of the students got wrong and this will lead to some board-work discussion to clear up any misunderstanding.

Boxer adds that he has identified numerous strengths with this approach. As well as encouraging retrieval practice, the combination of current and previous topics means that areas of study are spaced and interleaved. It is a straightforward process, which students understand well, and as all the questions and answers are available to the students, a high success rate is possible (we already know that retrieval challenge and retrieval success are both important). Another strength is how easily it has been adapted by other teachers. This is an activity where, once again, parents can be involved, as Boxer emails a copy of the roulette to students and parents.

Another benefit Boxer has described is that he has thoroughly enjoyed creating the roulettes as he states it has been so powerful for developing and deepening his pedagogical content knowledge, further enabling him to understand key components of the material he is teaching.

Boxer does recognise that there are some potential weaknesses to this approach as there can be no diagram questions, which is important in his subject, and no multiple-choice questions, and it does also rely on effective peer-assessment to a certain extent too.

You can see more Retrieval Roulette examples and read more of his fascinating posts about education on his teaching website www.achemicalorthodoxy.wordpress.com and you can follow Adam on Twitter @adamboxer1.

Retrieval Raffle

This may appear as a gimmicky activity but younger classes have responded well to this retrieval task. As students enter the classroom they select a random number from a jar/box/hat/tray (or anything you have available in your classroom). It can be a raffle ticket or simply a piece of paper with a number written on. On the board a list of topics, questions or keywords will be projected next to a number. The students then have to carry out a brain dump, answer the question or provide a definition of the word next to the number.

This is a short quick-fire task to promote retrieval and it adds a dimension of challenge as, unlike other activities, students don't get to pick what they retrieve, instead they have to do so based on the number on the raffle ticket they selected. This can be self assessed or peer assessed too.

If students have time and have completed the recall task, they could swap raffle tickets with a peer to complete another retrieval task. This could also be adapted to colours instead of numbers with students randomly selecting a coloured piece of paper or coloured token. Depending on your class and abilities, it may work better if the teacher allocated numbers/colours to students if the level of challenge varies considerably with each question or key term.

1. Norman	5. Baron	9. Housecarl	13. Shield wall
2. Bailey	6. Cavalry	10. Invasion	14. Monastery
3. Heir	7. Earl	11. Feudal system	15. Viking
4. Conqueror	8. Fyrd	12. Motte	16. Villein

Figure 16 Retrieval Raffle: Vocabulary

1. A person from Normandy in northern France	5. A powerful person who was given land by the King as part of the Feudal System	9. Full time and paid army, they were professional, well equipped and trained	13. A line or wall of shields used in battle to defend from attack
2. The large courtyard that was surrounded by a fence as part of a Motte & Bailey castle	6. The section of an army that were on horseback and often led the charge in a battle	10. When a country attacks another country to take over it	14. A religious building where monks lived nd worked
3. An individual who will inherit the throne	7. A very powerful noble man	11. The hierarchical system of dividing up the land	15. Invaders from countries such as Denmark, Sweden and Norway
4. A person who wins a country through war	8. Harold's part time army of soldiers	12. A large mound of earth/hill where the castle was built	16. A medieval peasant

Figure 17 Retrieval Raffle answers

TV quizzes in the classroom: A good or bad idea?

There are so many classic game shows that focus on quizzing, subsequently they naturally lend themselves to a retrieval practice activity. I would suggest doing so with caution, although I am not saying that popular quiz formats cannot be used in the classroom, but based on my classroom experiences here's my reflections and advice.

In the early years of my teaching I loved the quiz template for *Who Wants To Be A Millionaire?* As a trainee I discovered a free online template, it even included the show soundtrack and a selection of catchphrases read by Chris Tarrant. I could use this to create a multiple-choice quiz for my classes so I used it regularly.

The first error I made was that I often asked individuals to answer the question based on the 'hands up' approach and this did not involve everyone in the retrieval process. Another mistake was based on how the template was created: if a question were answered incorrectly, the player would go back to the beginning of the quiz and at the time I had no idea how to edit this, so I just accepted it as an annoying feature! Therefore, if a student had raised their hand and suggested a wrong answer I would ask if they were sure, encourage them to phone a friend or keep asking until the right answer was provided because I did not have time to go back to the beginning. Also, the musical introduction and Chris Tarrant's voice-over quickly lost its novelty appeal and actually took up precious and valuable learning time. Ultimately, this resource was more gimmickry than retrieval. However, a few small changes could change that.

Firstly, I am confident I would now be able to remove or edit the unnecessary sound effects and visuals to spend more time answering the actual questions. I would also ask students to use mini whiteboards as a way of engaging all learners and, as a result, providing retrieval opportunities for all. I would also think more carefully about the question design too as we know recognition with multiple-choice questions is easier than free recall I would create challenging questions and try to address or identify any misconceptions.

There are lots of popular game show templates to download online, examples I have seen include *Blockbusters*, *The Chase* and *The Million Pound Drop*. As long as we remember the key principles of retrieval practice and make sure education is our priority, not entertainment – removing any features to streamline the activity – then there can be a place for this style of quizzing in the classroom.

Summary

- We can take previously used resources, games and quizzes and adapt them for retrieval practice in the classroom.

- Retrieval practice is a great way to start a lesson, but it can be used as a strategy at any point in the lesson and learning process.

- Retrieval practice questions that are generic require more retrieval effort but this is not a bad thing as retrieval challenge is good, but we do want to make difficulties in the classroom desirable.

- When creating or using resources we need to consider and ask if they are **low effort, high impact**.

- There are many templates of popular and well-known quizzes that are often used in the classroom but we should be careful as they are designed for entertainment not education.

Recommended reading

What Every Teacher Needs to Know About Psychology by David Didau and Nick Rose

Powerful Teaching: Unleash the Science of Learning by Pooja K. Agarwal and Patrice M. Baine

Making Every Lesson Count: Six Principles to Support Great Teaching and Learning by Shaun Allison and Andy Tharby

What Does This Look Like in the Classroom? Bridging the Gap Between Research and Practice by Carl Hendrick and Robin Macpherson

Just Great Teaching: How to Tackle the Top Ten Issues in UK Classrooms by Ross Morrison McGill

CHAPTER 3:
RETRIEVAL PRACTICE AND THE SCIENCE OF LEARNING

The science of learning isn't just about retrieval practice, far from it. Instead the science of learning, also referred to as cognitive science or psychology, focuses on a wide range of strategies and techniques. Dunlosky emphasised that retrieval practice wasn't the only effective study strategy as he stressed the importance and impact of distributed/spaced practice too. Another benefit of retrieval practice is that this approach can be combined with other effective strategies and that is the main focus of this chapter.

Retrieval practice and spaced practice

When explaining spaced practice to my students I find the best way to do it is to suggest that instead of spending four hours studying the same topic in one sitting or session, it would be better to spread those four hours across four days instead. The same amount of time is being dedicated to learning, no more or no less, but the time is simply organised differently by being distributed. This may seem a difficult concept for learners to accept but the advice is based on spaced practice, regarded as one of the most effective and powerful revision strategies for students. By spreading studying out, it also encourages students to avoid crammed or mass practice (the opposite to spaced practice).

Agarwal and Baine explain that 'when students engage in retrieval practice but it's crammed all at once, learning isn't nearly as robust'.[1] This once again emphasises that whilst retrieval practice is effective we shouldn't consider it a singular or all-encompassing strategy. Retrieval is much more effective if it is repeated. Agarwal and Baine, further add that 'by returning to content every so often, students knowledge has had time to rest and be refreshed'.[2]

---

1. Baine, P. and Agarwal, P. K. (2019) *Powerful Teaching: Unleash the Science of Learning.* San Francisco, CA: Jossey-Bass.
2. Ibid.

Retrieval practice is an essential learning strategy and study habit. It is even more powerful and effective when combined with spaced practice. If students don't space out their revision and consolidation then it's likely they will resort to last minute mass practice and cramming, which is intense, stressful and not effective for long-term learning and retention. Students may argue that they believe there are short-term benefits of cramming but learning through cramming is temporary and shallow,[3] which isn't meaningful. Retrieval and spaced practice can be a winning combination when it comes to long-term learning.

Cramming is ineffective and can be anxiety inducing, this is when students revise for a very intense period of time just before the exam. In comparison to spaced practice, which can reduce stress and improve confidence with regular retrieval over a period of time. This approach requires students to plan their time carefully to ensure all subjects and topics within those subjects are covered in shorter chunks over a longer period of time. We can advise our students to divide up their revision into short manageable chunks of time, aiming for 20 to 30 minutes. Revision activities in this chapter, such as the revision clock, support this approach. It is important that students stop and take a break when they realise they are struggling to maintain focus and concentration. Dividing up revision into smaller, manageable sections will benefit students in the long term too as the revision they complete for mock and trial exams will stick for their final exams (unlike cramming).

Retrieval practice challenge grids (known as retrieval grids online) have become a widely shared and adapted resource – the positive feedback and response I have received from teachers and students has been very pleasing. This activity was inspired by the challenge grid in Chapter 2 but I shifted the focus of the questions to ensure coverage of content over a wider period of time, ranging from last lesson, last week, last term or month and further back.

---

3. Carpenter, S. K. and Agarwal, P. K. (2019) 'How to use spaced retrieval practice to boost learning'. Ames, IA: Iowa State University.

Retrieval grids

Describe the problems facing Germany in 1918	What does the term 'Dolchstoss' mean?	Who was involved in the Kapp Putsch?
Why was there opposition to the Weimar Republic?	What was Article 48?	What were the consequences of the French invasion of the Ruhr?
List two strengths and two weakness of the Weimar Constitution	Who put down the Spartacist uprising?	Why were the Weimar Republic known as the 'November criminals'?
Explain why Kaiser Wilhelm abdicated	Why did the French invade the Ruhr?	List four terms of the Treaty of Versailles

1 point - Last lesson   2 points - Last week   3 points - 2 weeks ago   4 points - Further back

Figure 1 Retrieval practice challenge grid

This task combines retrieval, spacing and interleaving. I tend to use the retrieval practice challenge grid at the start of a lesson, although it can be used at any point in a lesson, as other teachers have told me they prefer to use it at the end of a lesson. The example in figure 1 of a retrieval practice challenge grid was created as a homework task. You can also decide how much time you wish to dedicate to this activity, this will depend on how many questions are included in the grid and how feedback is provided. This task can easily be used in any subject and across all year groups, as the examples in the figures shown demonstrate.

The retrieval grid will contain several boxes and each box contains a question and is colour coded for the time when students first learned or encoded the concept. Retrieval practice challenge grids can also provide opportunities for feedback (as all retrieval practice tasks should in some form) the grid can be self or peer assessed and lead to classroom or teacher-led discussion of the content. Retrieval practice challenge grids are low or no stakes. There is the option to award points, but in order to be truly no-stakes the point system can be removed.

Even though I created this resource I have reflected and can recognise some weaknesses that I thought I would share. Firstly, trying to select questions from a week ago, two weeks ago, last month or last term can be time consuming and this task takes longer to prepare than most of the other tasks in this book. My advice would be to create a bank of questions that cover the topic, ones that can be copied and pasted onto the grid at different stages throughout the academic term/ year, depending on the point you are at as part of your curriculum or specification (as Adam Boxer did with his ready-made retrieval roulette questions, discussed in the previous chapter). For exam classes, a specification can be a good guide to support question design. Another alternative would be to write down three questions from a lesson as you go to make it more manageable and in the near (or distant) future you can revisit the questions you have previously recorded so you create a gradual question bank over time.

Another potential issue with the grid is that it can often take longer than ten minutes for students to complete and self-assess, therefore it is not always an ideal starter task, which was the main purpose when I originally created it. This issue can be easily overcome by reducing the amount of boxes used in the grid or it could be used as a lesson or revision activity instead of a starter task.

I did allow students to spend a whole lesson on a retrieval grid and this worked really well – I wasn't actually there in the lesson due to a planned absence but the feedback from the cover teacher and students were positive in addition to the fact that I checked their answers and self-corrections. I thought carefully about the work I would leave for my class to complete in my absence and I had prepared a retrieval grid so decided to set this as the task. This obviously took the pressure away from the cover teacher as they did not have to deliver a lesson outside of their subject knowledge and it provided time for thoughtful retrieval. The fact the class had the whole lesson meant that students could attempt all of the questions and the extra time allowed them to write more in-depth answers and also have the time to revisit the topics that the grid had highlighted as an area of weakness. I do try to avoid planned absences where possible but it does happen and this has proven itself as a good option.

Challenge grid examples

Thank you to the teachers who are referenced for allowing me to share examples of this resource in their subjects. There is a QR code at the back of this book where you can download free retrieval grid templates. Mark Anderson has kindly created templates for PowerPoint, Keynote, Google Slides and PDF formats on his website www.ictevangelist.com.

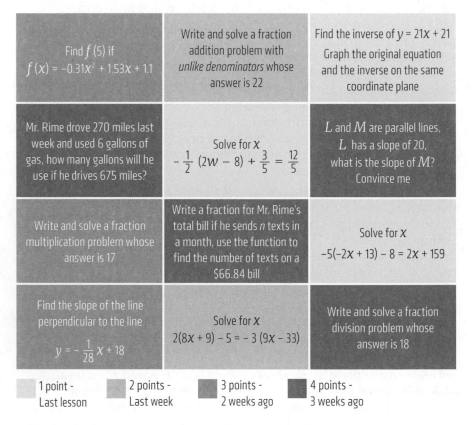

Figure 2 Maths retrieval practice challenge grid
Credit Nick Soderstrom (@NickSoderstrom)

What is coronary heart disease and what risk factors may increase the risk of developing coronary heart disease?	Can you give the different components of the blood and explain their structure and their function?	Can you define the processes of diffusion, osmosis and active transport?	Can you explain the structure of arteries, veins and capillaries and how this relates to their function?
Why do large organisms need a transport system?	Can you draw and label a bacterial and yeast cell?	How does clotting work?	Can you explain the cardiac cycle?
How is clotting necessary?	Can you explain how the heart rate changes during exercise and under the influence of adrenaline?	Can you draw a sketch diagram of the heart and label the vessels entering and leaving it?	Can you compare and contrast the parts of animal, plant, bacterial and yeast cells?

1 point - Last lesson

2 points - 2 weeks ago

3 points - 3 weeks ago

4 points - Way back

Figure 3 Science retrieval practice challenge grid
Science: Credit Jade Booth (@missjmbooth)

Rank the following in order of importance with reasoning for *Othello*: passion, malice, vulnerability.	Give two examples of *Othello* critical analysis or of *Othello* intertextuality.	How is artifice and reality depicted in *Othello*? Support with evidence.	Rank the following in order of importance with reasoning for *Streetcar*: passion, malice, vulnerability.	Which theme is the poker game most significant for: power, time or sensuality?
Give specific examples of Greek Mythology utilised in every text studied this year.	Explore Stella's position in the play with supporting quotes.	How significant is light and darkness in *A Streetcar Named Desire*?	State the importance of the title *History* and link to another poem.	How are men other than Iago and Othello presented in the play? Why?
How is Emilia presented throughout the play? How important is her role in the drama?	How are secrets presented in 'A Streetcar Named Desire'? Support your answer with evidence.	State two 'Poems of the Decade' that would reinforce themes of modernity.	Define 'Kitchen Sink Drama' with an example from *A Streetcar Named Desire*.	Give one contemporary intertextual quote to demonstrate views on Othello's race.
Explore the characterisation of Blanche in *A Streetcar Named Desire*.	Do any poems deal with a sense of 'rebirth'? If so, which? Ensure you have quotations.	'Iago is the central character of Othello above the eponymous hero', explore your perspective.	Name three poems where youth is an important theme and justify with quotations.	Which poems would most strongly tie to the themes of brutality? Give supporting evidence.

1 point - Last lesson   2 points - Last week   3 points - 2 weeks ago   4 points - 3 weeks ago

Figure 4 English literature retrieval practice challenge grid
English literature: Credit Jancke Schwartz (@awakenenglish)

If you are an English teacher I can highly recommend visiting Jancke Schwartz's website www.awakenenglish.com

Title: How does the structure of a population vary?

Starter		
How many points can you score in five minutes?		
State two factors that would change the birth rate of a county?	What is fertility rate? Why might it decrease as a country develops?	Why is the Scottish Highlands a sparsely populated area?
What is urbanisation? Why did it impact the population density and distribution in the UK?	Why does the death rate decrease as a country develops? Use an example for a bonus point.	Define infant mortality rate? What is the difference between that and child mortality rate?
Describe the growth of world population in the last 150 years. Try and include figures where possible.	Describe the difference between sparsely and densely populated. Can you name three examples of each in the UK?	Explain why HICs have a lower birth rate than LICs. Try and include more than one reason.
1 point - Last lesson	2 points - Last week	3 points - 2 weeks ago

Keywords
Youthful, ageing, structure, population pyramid

Homework
Choose a task off the menu

Figure 5 Geography retrieval practice challenge grid
Geography: Credit Jen Monk (@Jennnnnn_x)

Use your knowledge of design technology this term to answer or find out the answers to these key questions on the topic we have been studying.

What does the polymer mean? 1 mark	Explain what is meant by the term thermoplastic. 2 marks	Explain what is meant by the term thermoset plastic. 2 marks	What material could you use to prototype a design idea? 1 mark
What would you learn by prototyping a design idea? 2 marks	What does CAD stand for? Give an example. 2 marks	What are the advantages of using CAD? 2 marks	What does CAM stand for? Give an example. 2 marks
What are the advantages of using CAM? 2 marks	To make a product safe, what might the designer have to consider? 3 marks	What natural source is used to make plastic? 2 marks	What are the working properties of acrylic? 4 marks

12 marks = 30pts   18 marks = 40pts   25 marks = 50pts

Figure 6 Design technology retrieval practice challenge grid
Design technology: Credit @NED_DT

The version that is shown in figure 6 was designed for students to take home as a home learning task, which included previously covered work, and students were asked to write the answers on the grid in the spaces provided.

What can you remember about Robert Kett?	What year did Edward VI become king?	Explain the issue with enclosures.	How many men was Kett able to raise in the rebellion?
Who was Sir John Flowerdew?	What year was the *First Book of Common Prayer* published?	What was the 1547 Vagrancy Act?	Where did Kett's rebellion begin and mainly take place?
Explain the role of Edward Seymour, Duke of Somerset in the rebellion?	When did Kett's rebellion take place?	What were the main aims of the rebels?	What was the outcome of this rebellion?
Individuals	**Dates**	**Causes**	**Events**

Figure 7 History retrieval practice challenge grid

The history example about Kett's rebellion is one that I used with my A Level class. This example does not include points but instead focuses on different questions from a range of themes and categories, once again combining retrieval and spaced practice.

Another adaptation of the retrieval grid that focuses on retrieval and spaced practice is to only include four boxes that cover content from the last lesson, last week, last term and last year, as illustrated in figure 8. Each box can contain a question, task or heading to complete a mini brain dump. This is another simple strategy that proves effective for retrieval, identifying gaps in knowledge and interleaving topics.

Retrieval starter	
Last lesson:	Last week:
Last term:	Last year:

Figure 8 Retrieval starter

Retrieval practice and the dual coding theory

The influential work of Allan Paivio and his dual coding theory dates back to the 1960s and continued for the following decades, although I think it is fair to say there has been a recent resurgence and renewed interest in dual coding. Paivio and his colleagues conducted an experiment that demonstrated how students were able to recall more word pairs when they were associated with concrete visual images. The picture superiority effect refers to the ability to improve free verbal recall for materials presented as pictures instead of as words, but obviously we should not ignore the text. The dual coding theory suggests combing both text and visuals as the two formats provide two methods to remember information.

The term 'dual coding' refers to the technique and process of combining written text with visuals, or verbal communication with visuals, which working memory can deal with despite its limitations. Dual coding is sometimes referred to as 'multimedia learning' (or 'multimedia cognition' in research papers) because the material used and represented can be in multiple forms.

There are some simple adjustments we can make to our teaching that can have a big impact on the encoding, storage and retrieval stages. An obvious example of this is simply not talking over a slide with text when delivering a presentation. This was something I did unknowingly for many years and I am aware of many teachers that continue to do so. The alternatives to this are to allow students quiet time to read the text on screen or limit the amount of text, using visuals instead combined with a verbal explanation as we can't read and listen at the same time. This is explicitly linked to cognitive load theory and the idea that our working memory can only handle so much at a time. Reducing the text on a presentation and replacing it with headings and images does rely on teachers having strong subject knowledge, without heavy text to rely on, but this in itself is also a good thing.

As someone who has studied languages and was previously a teacher of Welsh second language, I can recall using images regularly to support students to learn new vocabulary in addition to regular retrieval. The popular app Duolingo uses visuals and regular testing to help language learners. I often feel there is so much other departments can learn from modern foreign languages teachers about the methods and strategies they use in the classroom.

De Bruyckere has explained the research showed that students who receive an explanation using both words and images remember more than the students who are taught the same content using just words or just images,[4] (it is important to note that the images used must have value and relevance to the content instead of simply improving the presentation). This is the dual channel theory, suggesting individuals will learn better using both strategies as there are two different ways of processing information.

The work of Oliver Caviglioli – a former special school headteacher turned designer – has also been incredibly helpful, informative and insightful in regards to dual coding and he is regarded as a leading expert in this field. In his masterful book *Dual Coding With Teachers*, Caviglioli writes that he believes dual coding has 'had a resurgence after its misunderstanding and association with learning styles'.[5] To further clarify, the references to visuals supporting learning is not a reference to people learning better because they are visual learners – as we know that has been well and truly debunked.

In his book, Caviglioli explores a range of key questions linked to dual coding in the classroom. These questions include what the strategies are and how they can be implemented, when should teachers incorporate dual coding and amongst other questions he addresses why teachers should be implementing this technique. Caviglioli explains the main benefits of using dual coding in our teaching approaches. He links this with the work of John Sweller and the limitations of

4. De Bruyckere, P. (2018) *The Ingredients for Great Teaching*. London: SAGE Publications.
5. Caviglioli, O. (2019) *Dual Coding With Teachers*. Woodbridge, Suffolk: John Catt Educational, p. 4.

our working memories. Below is an infographic based on the work of Caviglioli showing how the use of visuals is an effective teaching and learning strategy.

Graphic design can focus the **direct attention** of elements in a visual display, avoiding distractions and confusion.

Dual coding can support **managing cognitive load**.

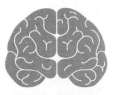

The clarity of graphic displays support the **learning of new information** in addition to making **links with prior knowledge**.

The clear organisation of information helps its **encoding into long-term memory** and the building of **meaningful schema**.

The more organised the information is when it is **encoded**, the easier it is to **retrieve** it and **transfer** to working memory.

The use of visuals can evoke **interest** and therefore **motivate** learners.

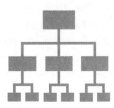

Figure 9 Benefits of dual coding based on the work of Oliver Caviglioli

Dual coding is similar to retrieval practice in the sense that teachers are keen to understand what this strategy looks like in the classroom. How can we apply and embed dual coding into our lessons to improve and impact teaching and learning? I have included a range of examples and tasks that involve the dual coding strategy, by combing written text and visual images with retrieval practice.

I have been using these strategies for many years but previously I encouraged students to include visuals from a presentation perspective, to enhance the visual appearance of work rather than being aware of the theory and benefits behind this technique. There is now a wealth of useful materials that can be easily accessed including videos, blog posts, podcasts and presentations shared by educators about how dual coding can be used effectively in the classroom.

Timelines

Timelines are an activity that work well with the study of chronology in history and politics. They can also be used in other subjects too, for example I have seen impressive timelines used in English literature and drama, illustrating the chronological order of events of a plot using both visuals and text. I should add that history isn't about recalling and listing a range of dates but chronology is an important aspect of the study of history. I don't always carry out timelines as a retrieval task because a timeline can help students during the encoding and consolidating stages to gain an overview of a period, to recognise change and continuity as well as help identify significant events.

Timelines can be a retrieval activity, simply remove the support and information. Depending on your class there are different ways this can be achieved. One example could be complete free recall with no guidance other than creating a timeline of events during a period of time and students do so purely from memory, but that could prove to be very difficult. Cues and support could be added if that is simply too difficult (challenge is good but remember we have to pitch it 'just right' with the Goldilocks approach to desirable difficulties). Key dates could be included at the start and end of the timeline or the timeline could include key dates without information.

Another method – although this is reducing the level of challenge and, therefore, the effectiveness of the retrieval – would be to create a sorting task where students have to put events in the correct chronological order. That will be easier and not likely to have the same impact so it is important to think and consider what your class and students are capable of and where you are in regards to the content being studied and retrieved.

Timelines are a fine example of dual coding as students can draw images to represent key events or individuals and combine the images with text and/or dates. The example in figure 10 is by an A Level student looking at art and culture in the Soviet Union, illustrating that this strategy can work well with older students in addition to younger students.

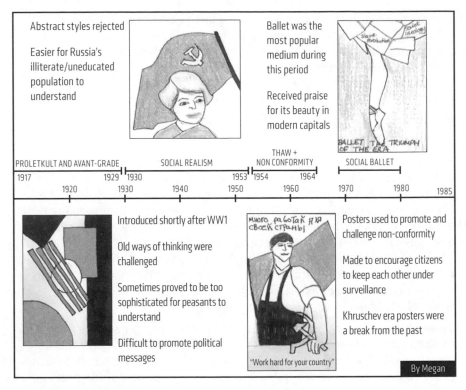

Figure 10 An A Level student using a timeline to look at art and culture in the Soviet Union

Diagrams and infographics

I like the simplicity yet effectiveness of diagrams and this is something I have only recently recognised the value of in the classroom. This task lends itself better to some subjects more than others, such as science, geography and maths, to identify and label different components. An example of a diagram I used in history was a picture of World War One trench that students had to label and annotate after they have spent time learning about the different features of a trench. I am now exploring how I could use diagrams more in my lessons.

Caviglioli commented that the internet has supported the popularity of infographics but they have actually been around for centuries.[6] I have created several digital infographics in this book, this did not involve retrieval practice because I had the research papers with me when I

---

6. Caviglioli, O. (2019) *Dual Coding With Teachers*. Woodbridge, Suffolk: John Catt Educational.

was creating the infographic summaries. However, infographics can be created when students write down information from memory with accompanying relevant images to enhance their points. Infographics combine visuals and text and can take many forms including explanatory, instructional or to summarise key information and data.

This fantastic example below is from a Year 8 student in science, kindly shared by Olly Lewis from The British International School, Abu Dhabi.

NUCLEAR FUELS

What is it?
It's a substance that is used to produce heat to power turbines. Heat is produced when nuclear fuels undergo the nuclear fission.

The main nuclear fuels are uranium and plutonium. These are radioactive metals. Unlike fossil fuels, nuclear fuels are not burnt to make energy. Instead, nuclear fission reactions in the fuels release energy.

The process of nuclear fission

fission product

fissionable nucleus

incident neutron

release of energy

Incident neutron

chain reaction

splitting of nucleus

Advantages
- Unlike fossil fuels nuclear fuels do not produce carbon dioxide or sulphur dioxide.
- This helps slow global warming down.

Disadvantages
- Fossil fuels and nuclear fuels are non-renewable energy resources.
- It must be stored safely.

Did you know?
20% of US electricity comes from nuclear energy

Figure 10 A science infographic by a Year 8 student

Retrieval practice with memory mind maps

Mind maps or concept maps (also referred to as spider diagrams) are a well-known technique that tend to be used as a classroom strategy in combination with notes or a textbook during the encoding stages of learning new content. This can also be a retrieval activity too. A study was carried out by Blunt and Karpicke (2014) titled 'Learning with retrieval-based concept mapping'.[7] The results of the study showed that 'practicing retrieval, either by creating concept maps or by writing down the material in paragraph format, enhanced long-term learning more than completing the same tasks as study activities'. This research illustrated that creating a mind map with notes is not an inherently good strategy but when combined with retrieval practice, it is more challenging and therefore more effective.

Another teacher from the AISC 2018 workshop was Kay McCabe, Head of Humanities and teacher of Geography. Mind mapping from memory is a strategy that Kay uses with her classes regularly. Kay spoke about this during her workshop and, on a teaching and learning website that she hosts with her colleagues, Kay explains how she uses memory mind maps in her classroom:

> I have used mind mapping in a number of ways as part of retrieval practice. When planning out my units for Geography IGCSE, I discussed with a colleague the tendency for us all to get so bogged down with getting through the content that we don't spend enough time thinking about how we can ensure that learners retain the information that we are teaching them. With content heavy IGCSE curriculums this had become a common problem across the humanities department. One strategy I have been trialling with my learners this year is mind mapping at the beginning of every half term. A new mind map every term to cover the units that we had covered in the previous terms learning and so on and so forth.
>
> I have also used mind mapping as part of a revision lesson. I have written out the key ideas for each unit on paper and asked the learners to complete a carousel, recording down what they know and understand about each of the key ideas, encouraging keywords, definitions, links, examples and case studies. Each learner was given a different colour pen so I could see everyone's contribution. Once the activity had been completed we then examined it for any misconceptions or misinformation and cross referenced it against their notes to identify gaps in knowledge and understanding.'

You can follow Kay on Twitter @KayMc100.

---

7. Blunt, R. J. and Karpicke, J. D. (2014) 'Learning with retrieval-based concept mapping', *Journal of Educational Psychology* 106 (3) pp. 849-858.

Cartoon and comic strips

Cartoon and comic strips can be another classroom technique to combine dual coding and retrieval practice to demonstrate a sequence, story or events. This allows topics to be broken down into chunks and encourages the students to think hard about the key facts or points in addition to illustrating what they are able to recall. I have found that this has allowed students to be really creative and it has led to some impressive pieces of work in addition to supporting their learning.

Take the example in figure 12 by one of my former students Jesse, who was in Year 7 at the time. The illustrations alone provide an accurate overview of the Battle of Stamford Bridge in 1066 but the captions further enhance and support this explanation of events. Knowledge and understanding of retrieval practice is further enhanced when we combine it with knowledge of other research informed and innovative strategies for the classroom. Eventually, the teaching profession will (hopefully) reach a point where these techniques have become the norm and an essential part of our lesson and curriculum planning.

Figure 11 Battle of Stamford Bridge cartoon by Jesse

Summary

- Retrieval practice should become embedded as part of our classroom planning, practice and routines but it is only one tool in our educational toolkit.

- Retrieval practice is more powerful when combined with spaced (or distributed) practice.

- Dual coding refers to the technique of combining images with text and can be combined with retrieval practice for a wide range of tasks and activities.

- Understanding these different approaches is essential to successful and varied learning.

- There is now a vast amount of easy to access and practical research summaries, books and resources to inform us about the different areas of the science of learning.

Recommended reading

Dual Coding with Teachers by Oliver Caviglioli

Stop Talking, Start Influencing: 12 Insights From Brain Science to Make Your Message Stick by Jared Cooney Horvath

Understanding How We Learn: A Visual Guide by Yana Weinstein and Megan Sumeracki with Oliver Caviglioli

Psychology in the Classroom: A Teacher's Guide to What Works by Marc Smith and Jonathan Firth

Memorable Teaching: Leveraging memory to build deep and durable learning in the classroom by Peps Mccrea

CHAPTER 4: RETRIEVAL PRACTICE AND REVISION STRATEGIES

It is really important that we recognise retrieval practice is an essential revision strategy but – as shown throughout this book – it isn't *just* a revision strategy to be used as exams approach. Instead it should be used throughout the year as a regular part of the learning process. It's also important to understand that retrieval practice alone is not enough to ensure success for our students.

There are many factors that have to be taken into consideration (some outside of the teacher's control) and the infographic below illustrates the importance of retrieval practice when combined with other factors.

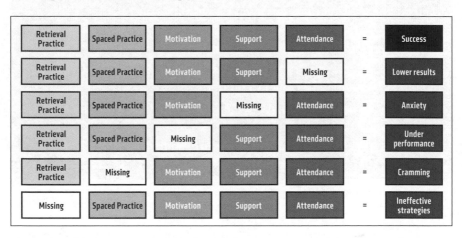

Retrieval Practice	Spaced Practice	Motivation	Support	Attendance	=	Success
Retrieval Practice	Spaced Practice	Motivation	Support	Missing	=	Lower results
Retrieval Practice	Spaced Practice	Motivation	Missing	Attendance	=	Anxiety
Retrieval Practice	Spaced Practice	Missing	Support	Attendance	=	Under performance
Retrieval Practice	Missing	Motivation	Support	Attendance	=	Cramming
Missing	Spaced Practice	Motivation	Support	Attendance	=	Ineffective strategies

Figure 1 A recipe for effective learning

The infographic in figure 1 that I created is based on some of the key areas that can impact the process and outcome when it comes to revision and exams. There are other factors that can be included and, as always, context is key. The different and combined factors are crucial to attainment and achievement, and the potential impact if one of the factors is missing can be very damaging and detrimental.

A teacher can educate students about the science of learning, ensure effective strategies are in place with lots of support and attendance could also be perfect but if the student doesn't try or has a fixed mindset then it is unlikely they will achieve their full potential. This can lead to serious underperforming with disappointing results, which can prove very frustrating for teachers and parents. This lack of effort and negative approach to learning can be a source of frustration at a later date, once students have completed their exams, because on reflection they know that they could have done better if they applied themselves and simply tried harder.

If a student is lacking self-motivation or has a poor attitude towards learning then it is unlikely they will achieve their potential (although this is not always true). The term motivation could be replaced with effort, mindset or general work ethic. Despite the importance of a positive attitude towards learning, cognitive scientist Daniel Willingham has identified in his well-known book, *Why Don't Students Like School? A Cognitive Scientist Answers Questions About How The Mind Works and What It Means For The Classroom*, that actually 'wanting to remember has little or no effect',[1] therefore the other factors are necessary too.

Attendance is a very difficult area for teachers, middle and senior leaders as it is often outside of our control. Low attendance can be very problematic as it can lead to lower results due to gaps in knowledge and can also create workload issues for teachers as they must support students to catch up on missed work.

Another issue with poor attendance is confusion for students, (depending on how many lessons/days/weeks missed) as this can lead to misconceptions and misunderstanding. An example being that, if a student were absent during a series of lessons about Henry VIII's decision to break with Rome, then his decision to close down the monasteries will not be fully understood as the context is absolutely essential. Resources such as knowledge organisers or a Virtual Learning Environment (such as Google Classroom or Firefly) can help students who have experienced absence or have gaps in their knowledge and understanding due to absence, but ultimately these resources cannot replace the teacher.

---

1. Willingham, D. T. (2010) *Why Don't Students Like School? A Cognitive Scientist Answers Questions About How The Mind Works And What It Means For The Classroom.* San Francisco, CA: Jossey-Bass, p. 58.

What can we do about this issue of attendance? Unfortunately, as with everything in education, there is no magic solution. There are some attendance issues that can be avoided, such as holidays and trips but other cases such as illness, injury or even bereavement do require everyone involved being as supportive as possible. It is also important that the Senior Leadership Team publish an academic calendar with any interruptions to the timetable as soon as possible so that teachers can factor this into their curriculum and lesson planning. Unexpected events do happen, such as a snow day or a strike, but it is imperative that both students and parents fully understand the importance of attendance at school. Every lesson really does count.

Finally, as we know, support is of paramount importance in a school environment and not just during the exam season, although that can be a very intense and stressful period. There has been a growing awareness and discussion and more media coverage about the negative impact of examinations on student mental and physical health.

I was on a panel at the Edinburgh Fringe Festival discussing the topic 'Generation Z Mental Health Crisis' in August of 2019. There was a clear agreement and consensus – unsurprisingly – that support is vital. Students often have a close support network around them in schools, from subject teachers to middle and senior leaders and pastoral provision that is in place. Parental support is also very important too. If students are equipped with strong subject knowledge in addition to a good understanding of effective revision strategies then this can provide support and increased confidence too. These factors are more important than 'wellbeing bags' with chocolates, tea bags and post-it notes (whilst those ideas do come with good intentions and are appreciated by students) and our support has to be on-going and long term.

Road map

This activity can be completed as a revision task or in lesson to review content from a lesson or several lessons. The road map layout lends itself well to subjects that deal with chronology or sequencing as it is very similar to a timeline, but it doesn't have the focus on key dates. The road map task does not have to link to chronology because the focus of the task is to provide an overview of a specific unit, module or topic from start to finish – once again linked with spaced practice.

As a history teacher I have used this with Year 7 classes and A Level students for both breadth and depth aspects. All that is required is a start and an end point, then students have to fill in the rest, using information that they can retrieve from memory. Students were given the template with simple instructions and then time to recall and write down as much as they could. I shared this with a colleague and they used it in drama, asking students to add the significant events from the play *The Blood Brothers* on the road map from memory; thus providing both an opportunity for retrieval and to check understanding of key events and themes studied. Once again, this is very useful for identifying gaps in knowledge and in addition to showing what students can recall confidently and accurately.

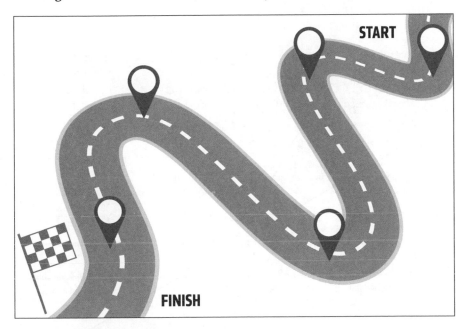

Figure 2 Retrieval practice road map

Revision clocks by Becky Russell

A revision clock can be used alongside notes to provide summaries and condense notes, but to make this a revision and retrieval activity then no notes are allowed. This is basically a template to provide 12 mini brain dumps where students get five minutes to write as much as they can from memory about a specific topic. This is good for retrieval and also for identifying areas of strength and weakness. The teacher can create the headings to go into each section of the revision clock as shown in figure 3, or alternatively students could use these independently and break down a topic or unit themselves. This is fitting for students who may struggle with time organisation as they have to restrict themselves to five minutes per section (you could edit the template and reduce the sections to ten, 15 or 20 minutes chunks for more depth, but I do prefer the five minute blocks). I have used this resource as part of spaced practice too, providing an opportunity to revisit previous content. I instruct students to write in two different colour pens. One colour will show all the information they have been able to retrieve from memory and in another colour will show the additional notes they have added to again make it very clear where the gaps in knowledge are. Download the free template and retrieve! [2]

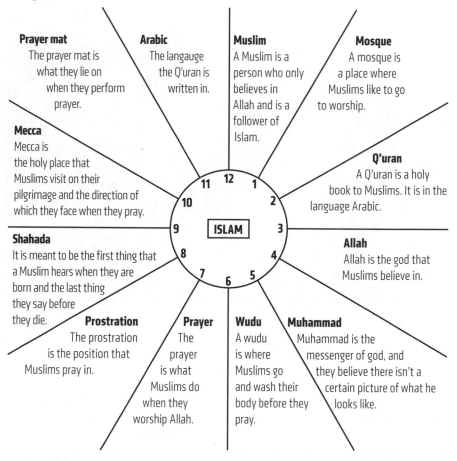

Figure 3 Revision clocks: Islam

For more creative ideas by Becky follow her on Twitter @teachgeogblog.

2. You'll find this in the Resources chapter.

Roll and retrieve grid

This is another classic resource for the classroom that is very adaptable and are known as learning grids or 6x6 grids. In regards to low effort, high impact, this resource can require significant effort. The main reason for that is the fact that the grid contains 36 boxes and therefore requires 36 questions! Learning grids, or 6x6 grids, is an idea originally credited to Steve Bowkett and I first discovered this activity in the popular book *Outstanding Teaching: Engaging Learners* by Andy Griffith and Mark Burns. I have adapted this idea in many ways and many to include retrieval.

The grid consists of 36 boxes, six numbers across and six numbers down, as shown in figure 4. A set of dice for the class is also required to use the grids. In pairs or small groups, students roll a set of dice once, as they will need a number to use both vertically and horizontally. They then answer the question in that specific box, hence 'roll and retrieve'!

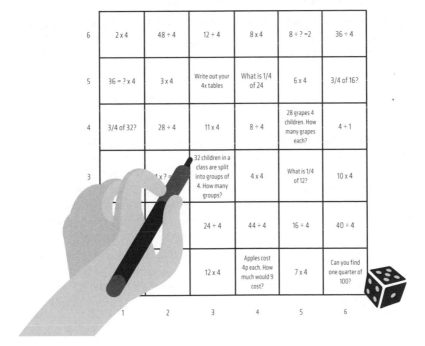

	1	2	3	4	5	6
6	2 x 4	48 ÷ 4	12 ÷ 4	8 x 4	8 ÷ ? =2	36 ÷ 4
5	36 = ? x 4	3 x 4	Write out your 4x tables	What is 1/4 of 24	6 x 4	3/4 of 16?
4	3/4 of 32?	28 ÷ 4	11 x 4	8 ÷ 4	28 grapes 4 children. How many grapes each?	4 ÷ 1
3		4 x ? =	32 children in a class are split into groups of 4. How many groups?	4 x 4	What is 1/4 of 12?	10 x 4
2			24 ÷ 4	44 ÷ 4	16 ÷ 4	40 ÷ 4
1			12 x 4	Apples cost 4p each. How much would 9 cost?	7 x 4	Can you find one quarter of 100?

Figure 4 Roll and retrieve grid

Thinking and linking grid

A thinking and linking grid was another way I adapted the original 6x6 learning grid and shows how retrieval practice can be used for making connections and exploring links and themes within a topic. This doesn't have to be a revision style activity but it will require students to have an overview of a topic in order to make the connections using their subject knowledge and understanding.

In pairs, or small groups, students roll the dice to get the coordinates both horizontal and vertical to have their first box. In the box will be a keyword or image, both work well in my experience but the key term helps with vocabulary retrieval and development. They repeat that action so that they can make a link between the words or images in the two boxes they have randomly selected with the dice. This can be challenging as some links are more obvious than others. Students can explain the link between the two boxes verbally with one another or could write down the links.

I originally shared this idea in *Love to Teach*, with two history examples from my classroom but I knew this activity had the potential to work well in other subjects. After reading my book, English teacher Stuart Pryke @SPryke2 created his own version focusing on *A Christmas Carol* for his GCSE English class, as shown in figure 5. If the two key terms were 'poverty' and 'workhouse' the student would explain the link between the two in the context of the text they are studying.

Every time I have used this activity I have been surprised and impressed by the links and connections students make as there are the obvious links but it provides learners with the opportunity to not only retrieve information but also establish deep connections too. There could be times where the links are very tenuous or it is simply too difficult – at that point I often have a class discussion to see if together we can make a link but, if not, students can have another attempt, however I do try to avoid this. Students could also work together to discuss links between their connecting terms or images. This is a very adaptable resource that does make students think hard and as Willingham has famously stated: 'Memory is the residue of thought'.

	1	2	3	4	5	6
1	Scrooge	Light	Tiny Tim	Marley's chains	Memory	Forgiveness
2	Family	The Ghost of Christmas Yet to Come	Scrooge as a school boy	Martha Cratchit	Fan	Peter Cratchit
3	Gratitude	Christmas	Reform	Poverty	Cold	The Ghost of Christmas Past
4	Marley's ghost	The charity collectors	Bob Cratchit	Ignorance and Want	Mrs Cratchit	Generosity
5	Hope	The Ghost of Christmas Present	Compassion	The workhouse	Redemption	Fezziwig
6	Repentance	Isolation	Belle	Responsibility	Fred	Guilt

Links made

Box 1	Box 2	Link between the two

Figure 5 Thinking and linking grid: *A Christmas Carol*

Flash cards

Flash cards are a very useful revision activity for many reasons. They work across all subjects, they can be used with the recall of facts, figures, statistics, dates, quotes, definitions and more. They are a very simple revision strategy for learners to use. Although popular amongst students as a revision strategy, how effective flash cards actually are depends entirely on how they are used. I have seen collections of beautiful flash cards with detailed notes and diagrams filling each card. This does show students are revising but more often they are simply copying their notes onto cards and re-reading, which we know is not the most effective of study techniques. Regardless of what the name implies, flash cards don't need to be flashy.

When students create flash cards with questions on one side and answers on the other (or keywords and definitions on the back) this promotes self or pair testing to ensure active recall – retrieval practice is taking place. It is vital students include the answers when creating flash cards because this provides instant feedback and guidance. This feedback also informs students where the gaps in their knowledge are that they need to return to and focus on. Using flash cards for questioning and answering is simply the best way to use flash cards. It is important that students consciously recall the answer to the question on their flash cards, either verbally or through writing. The reason for this being that many students can struggle to self-test. They may see a question and think they know the answer and, before consciously recalling it, they have turned over to read the answer and told themselves they knew it, but in reality they just *recognised* the answer instead of actually going through the process of recalling. Students should say the answer out loud or write the answer down before checking their answers. It's not difficult to grasp, but it surprising how flash cards can be used in different ways, varying in degrees of effectiveness!

Students can also use dual coding when creating flash cards, combining images with their questions and/or answers, but it's important to remember if students have an image or diagram to accompany a question then that is essentially providing a clue and making the question easier to recall and answer. They could combine their answer with an illustration making it more memorable, they do not see the image with the question but instead – when generating an answer – they can refer back to both the text and image to help them recall the information.

As mentioned in Chapter 2, Quizlet, the largest online flash card site, is a great online tool for creating digital flash cards. There are other apps and websites available that we can use or recommend for students to create their own flash cards on their devices so that they always have their flash cards with them, assuming that their device is also always with them too, of course! Many of the digital flash cards apps and websites have pre-prepared flash cards made by other users, ranging from teacher or student created flash cards. These can work well for retrieval but they are not always specific to an exam topic, unit or specification so it may be a better suggestion to encourage students to create their own, although they may need guidance as to how to do this.

Here are some popular flash card apps available across all devices. All are free but do require the user to set up an account using an email address, so it is worth checking the age requirements before recommending any apps to your students:

- **StudyBlue**. You can search for ready-made flash cards by typing a specific topic or question and viewing what flash cards are public across a wide range of different subjects. The user can also create their own flash cards on this app very easily. The user can include a question and answer or term and definition as well as an option to upload images from a camera roll. The user can make their flash cards public or private. There are options to create multiple-choice, free recall, fill in the blanks or true or false questions.

- **Brainscape**. Again, the user can find flash cards or create their own. If the user wants to use ready-made flash cards then there is the option to preview a deck first then take the quiz. There is also the option for the user to reflect and rate how well they knew the answer from 1 ('not at all') to 5 ('perfectly').

- **Flash Cards Flashcards Maker**. A very basic app with some useful features, but some additional features will cost within the app. The user creates their own decks of flash cards that they can easily share with their peers or sync to their iCloud account. Flash cards can be randomly shuffled too.

My flash card top tips

- Use different colour flash cards for different subjects, such as green for science and pink for history, or use the different colours for different categories or topics. Colour coding is purely to help with organisation, not recall.

- Aim to include one question per flash card or limit the amount of questions. This is to avoid confusion and make it explicitly clear where the gaps in knowledge are. The focus should always be on the questions and answers, not copying and re-reading. Sometimes my students include a relevant bonus question, allowing an opportunity for further elaboration on the original question. The flash card may not even require a question but instead a prompt – whether a word or phrase – that students can use to recall as much as they can before flipping the card to check the accuracy of their answers.

■ Don't make questions on flash cards too ambitious. I am not implying that flash cards questions should be easy, but an essay style question – such as: 'How accurate is it to say that Stalin's use of terror in the 1930s was fundamentally similar to Lenin's use of terror in the years 1918–1924?' – is obviously not suitable. The answer to that complex question will not fit on the back of a flash card! Instead the question could be phrased 'Summarise the main features of Stalin's use of terror in the 1930s', again it's complex but more practical for flash cards by breaking the question down and making it more manageable. Extended questions should be used for practice essays or essay planning; flash cards should be used as one method, but it's not the only method of revision. Keep flash cards concise and clear.

■ We should remind students flash cards don't need to be stylish or expensive. Flash cards can be purchased cheaply as a pack (some retail outlets being far more cheaper than others so I would suggest visiting a local discount shop), or alternatively sections of cards can be cut and divided into flash cards or post-it notes can be used. Easy.

■ Creating flash cards that cover content of a two-year exam course at GCSE or A Level can be overwhelming. Students should consider creating flash cards from the beginning of the academic year and continue as the course progresses. Eventually, they will have created a collection of useful flash cards and as the exams approach they will be so pleased that they did so that they can dedicate their time and efforts to the retrieval process.

■ Encourage parents or peers to get involved with flash cards by asking the questions and checking answers. Often parents are keen to support their children with revision and this is a way that is possible and will ensure retrieval is taking place with students verbally answering questions.

■ I tell students to shuffle and mix up their revision flash cards when using them in case the students begin to recall facts in a specific sequence; this isn't helpful in the long term.

- We should remind students to combine flash cards with spaced practice, instead of quizzing for large periods of time, space it out over a period – not to use flash cards for last minute cramming.

Flash cards with the Leitner system

The Leitner system (originally proposed by the German science journalist Sebastian Leitner in the 1970s) is another useful way of using flash cards, combining retrieval and spaced practice. The focus of this system is to help students revisit the cards/topics that they have previously struggled with, until they can retrieve that information with ease and confidence. There are different variations of the Leitner system, but the main method I have seen used regularly by teachers – and that I share with my students – involves using three boxes (this can be a tray or a plastic wallet, something to store the flash cards). This system does rely on students using their flash cards on a regular basis for self-quizzing during the week so commitment is required but we know effective learning is effortful.

Once students have their flash cards on a Monday they will attempt to answer the questions or provide definitions of key terms, depending on the tasks, and whether they answer correctly or incorrectly will result in which box the flash card goes to. If students answer correctly the flash card will go in the box, labelled box two Tuesday and Thursday, meaning they will return to the flash card on Tuesday and Thursday. If the student cannot answer the question or provides an incorrect answer, they put the flash card in box one, the everyday box, meaning they have to keep repeating the flash card to support with the retrieval process.

The following day students will repeat the process. If they still cannot answer the flash cards from box one they remain there, but if they have now mastered that flash card it will move to box two. If students answer a question from box two incorrectly then it goes back to box one. When students are able to correctly answer the questions in box two they will be moved to box three, only to be revisited on Friday. This process will continually be repeated, either with the same flash cards or for different subjects and topics. It is a good way to identify gaps in knowledge and ensure that those knowledge gaps are returned to and revisited with retrieval again.

To find out more about the Leitner System I highly recommend watching a video on Youtube called 'The Leitner System', delivered by primary school teacher Jon Hutchinson.[3] In this tutorial style video, Hutchinson explains

---

3. Hutchinson, J. (2018) 'The Leitner System', *Youtube* [Video] 1 February. Retrieved from: www.bit.ly/2K1Ppjs

how he has used this system with his Year 4 class. I think it's brilliant that he is using this strategy with young learners. To create the flash cards, he uses the class knowledge organiser, which contains key facts and definitions linked to the unit they are studying. This is a very helpful and clear explanation as to how this strategy can support students with their learning and worth showing to your colleagues and students and parents too in order to involve everyone in the retrieval process.

Retrieve, record and reflect

The majority of our students (depending on which age group you teach) will have access to smartphones or tablet devices. Taking photos and filming is something that a lot of young people do and it's usually to post on social media. However, there is potential to use a simple recording device for retrieval practice.

Students simply have to record themselves (this could be using audio or video on a smart device) retrieving information from memory with no notes or script about a specific topic or unit. Some students find it much easier or enjoy recalling information verbally and this provides them with an opportunity to do so. Students can then also listen back or watch their retrieval recording. This again shows students what they know whilst identifying gaps in their knowledge or areas they may have struggled or lack confidence. Listening back to it and comparing against their notes is a useful form of reflection.

Meet the 'Study Tubers'

When we think about influencers in education we probably refer to the teachers, leaders, consultants and government advisors that have a large following online and are making an impact with their contributions in this field. Greta Thunberg is a young activist for climate change from Sweden that has quickly attracted a lot of media attention and a very large following. You have probably heard of Thunberg but did you know there's also a new generation of student educational influencers that have huge followings online with large audiences known as the 'Study Tubers'? Young people are following these Study Tubers, watching their videos online, viewing their posts and stories on Instagram and Snapchat, and listening to their podcasts too.

Who are these Study Tubers? My A Level students – who are subscribed to and regularly watch videos by Study Tubers – filled me in on the phenomenon in a lesson. I was surprised I wasn't familiar with any of these individuals yet they had such large followings and influence.

I was curious to find out what advice and support they were offering to other students and whether they were familiar with the science of learning, especially the power of retrieval practice.

According to a report by the National Citizen Service (NCS) one in five teenagers are now using Study Tubers to help aid revision for their GCSEs. The report added that Study Tubers offer social support for students who feel isolated and that 41% of those asked say that their parents try hard but don't know how to help with revision, and subsequently they have turned to the internet for help.[4] The main aims of the Study Tuber videos are to support students with advice on how to be more productive and organised in addition to sharing revision and study strategies such as the 'study with me' videos, where Study Tubers film themselves studying (they will often speed up videos using a timelapse feature).

Jade Bowler (known as UnJaded Jade by her subscribers and followers) is about to begin university and she has stated that: 'There can be a lot of stigma around studying being nerdy and not trying hard is more cool, which I think is really silly.' Of course, as educators, we agree with this message. In addition to the beauty, lifestyle and gaming videos and tutorials, there is now a Study Tuber online community focusing on learning, studying and general aspects of being a student, either in school or university.

Study Tuber	YouTube subscribers	Twitter followers	Instagram followers
Jade Bowler – 'UnJaded Jade'	379K	22.9K	125K
Ruby Grainger	369K	7,377	77.4K
Jack Ben Edwards	154K	44.5K	47.1K
Ibrahim Mohammed – 'Ibz Mo'	115K	13.8K	27.4K

Figure 6 The Study Tubers

4. Turner, C. (2019) 'One in five teenagers now using "Study Tubers" to help them revise for GCSEs, survey shows', *The Telegraph* [Online] 4 April. Retrieved from: www.bit.ly/2IbSdwO

This table in figure 6 shows an overview of the profiles of some of the leading Study Tubers to help you to gain insight as to how influential they have become. These figures are accurate at the time of writing, but I am sure that even by the time of publication their followers will have increased as the Study Tubers continue to grow with popularity and reach wider audiences. This really is incredible: young people supporting, inspiring and motivating one another and becoming educational influencers in their own right.

I have watched several videos posted by Jack Ben Edwards and it is clear he is a really hardworking, dedicated and enthusiastic learner. I've no doubt his audiences like his personality and sense of humour too. Not all of his posts and vlogs are linked to education – there are others dedicated to travel, mental health and even *Love Island*!

One of his most popular videos is titled '10 Things I did to get A* A* A* in my A Levels (A* Revision Tips and Techniques 2018)', and it is really interesting to listen to revision advice from a student perspective. In contrast to that video is a very personal, honest and open vlog that I think can help students pastorally, where Jack shares his experience of the Oxbridge application process and how he dealt with the rejection from Oxford University. This demonstrates and promotes both reflection and resilience.

Below are some of the methods and techniques Jack has shared online:

- Jack is very organised. He explains how he creates revision to-do lists, taken from examination or module specifications then working through the list ticking once covered. He is very specific with his exam revision planning. He offers advice about being sensible and realistic by setting short and long-term goals. He uses Excel to create weekly revision schedules and also recommends free apps such as the Homework App and My Study Plan that have also helped him to prepare during exam season. This has led to him launching his own company with academic planners for students.

- Jack emphasises the importance of breaking down topics into smaller, manageable chunks. He does this through summarising and condensing his notes. This also prevents revision material and content from becoming overwhelming.

- Jack uses a range of strategies from timelines, flash cards for testing, memory mind maps and creating essay or exam answer plans.

■ Despite the fact that Jack clearly uses social media a lot as an influencer, he does recognise and discuss the importance of a digital detox and self-regulation with screen time. Jack explains how he blocks distractions to prevent procrastination when studying. He suggests a range of apps such as Self-Control which allows the user to restrict specific websites or apps for a certain period of time. There is also the screen time feature available on iOS, which can monitor and limit screen time too. Jack even hides his phone away in another room, which might sound odd, but removing the phone completely can be a good idea! A study carried out in 2014 found that even the presence of a cell phone and what it might represent (such as social communication and updates) can be similarly distracting and have negative consequences and 'that the mere presence of a phone may be sufficiently distracting to produce diminished attention and deficits in task performance, especially for tasks with greater attentional and cognitive demands' – just the presence of a mobile phone led to 20% reduction in attention, concentration and performance![5]

■ I was initially concerned when I saw highlighters appear in a revision 'study with me' style video. However, after listening to Jack I was pleased to learn he was using highlighters not to learn material but simply colour code different categories for example in history he would use different colours for key dates, key terms, locations, statistics and so on, to identify the different factors that need to be studied. This is a good use of highlighters but this approach must then be followed by retrieval practice and the realisation that colour coding alone will not transfer or retrieve information to and from long-term memory.

■ It was great to listen to Jack tell his audience to look after themselves. This is a strong message that teachers, leaders and parents often repeat to students, especially during the exam period but this message being echoed from a fellow student can be very powerful for young people and helps break the stigma and silence around mental health issues. Jack recommends blogs, websites and charities that can help with stress, anxiety and pressure, as well as sharing ways he looks after his own mental and physical health.

■ Jack does not space his revision (although he should) and he explains why – this sums up perfectly why students can be reluctant to

5. Thornton, B., Faires, A., Robbins, M. and Rollins, E. (2014) 'The mere presence of a cell phone may be distracting: Implications for attention and task performance', *Social Psychology* 45 (6) pp. 479-488

embrace both spaced and retrieval practice. Jack recalled when he was studying for his history A Level exam and when he revising different modules one after another he felt this was 'muddled'. Therefore, he would dedicate specific days to specific units or topics. This sounds logical but as we know this is not what the research suggests is effective. It may not be as comfortable but Jack should now try to space out and interleave his revision.

■ A lot of students listen to music whilst revising, Jack explained in one of his videos he listens to music without lyrics, as songs with lyrics are often distracting. Music can certainly be motivating –we know that from a gym playlist or when our favourite song plays on the radio – but this does not mean that music can be motivational in a learning context. There has been research carried out about the impact of listening to music whilst studying. A study found that students who revised in a quiet environment with no music performed over 60% better in an exam than their peers who revised listening to music that had lyrics. Students who revised to music without lyrics did better than those who revised listening to music with lyrics.[6] This is insightful and something else we should share with our students.

I do think it is amazing that there are young, studious and driven students creating content for other students to help with their studies and revision. The sheer dedication and commitment shown to studying makes these influencers sensible role models to young people – showing that students do need to invest time and effort into their studies and take responsibility and ownership for learning.

However, despite the efforts and popularity of the Study Tubers, it is clear that students do still need specific and explicit guidance (in addition to support) from their teachers in regards to retrieval practice and the science of learning. Hopefully the next generation of student influencers will be very familiar with the science and language of learning, focusing on retrieval practice, spaced practice, dual coding and more. Ask your students if they are familiar with the Study Tubers community. It might lead to an interesting conversation with your class about the science of learning and revision routines. The next Study Tuber could be a student from your classroom, spreading the word about the science of learning! If you haven't seen any of the Study Tubers videos then you should check them out to see for yourself.

---

6. Busch, B. and Watson, E. (2019) *The Science of Learning: 77 Studies That Every Teacher Needs to Know.* Abingdon, Oxon: Routledge, p. 39.

Case study: Getting parents involved with retrieval practice using quizzing booklets by Emily Folorunsho

A lot of teachers are investing time creating booklets for their students to use. The benefits of booklets are that they can be personalised and adapted for different classes and topics taught. A textbook can be a great resource for teachers, but the quality of textbooks can vary significantly. Textbooks tend to include a variety of tasks for students to complete but again the quality of the tasks in textbooks can be questionable. If you are able to find a textbook with a good level of depth, detail and appropriate activities then that really can be an excellent go-to resource for both teachers and students.

Emily Folorunsho, a history teacher and lead practitioner based in London, has created a booklet that isn't just for her students but was created with the aim to involve parents in the retrieval and revision process too. Here Emily describes the booklets she has designed, how she has shared them and evaluated the impact they had:

> Teaching the new GCSE has been difficult for students due to the vast amount of content. Students on average sit around 30 examination papers in the summer as each subject has around two to three units. Consequently, students can no longer get away with cramming, especially the low and mid-ability learners. After coming across many blogs, books and research about retrieval practice, I decided to implement regular low-stakes quizzing, but with a twist.

> The Education Endowment Foundation in their Teaching and Learning Toolkit (2018) revealed that 'increasing parental engagement in [...] schools had on average two to three months' positive impact'. As a result, I began to think of ways to marry up retrieval practice with parental engagement. Having younger siblings in primary education, I saw that primary schools utilise parental involvement by making parents sign their child's reading journal after their child has read to them. However, I have noticed that as children get older and progress into secondary education, parental involvement and engagement declines. This is due to many reasons such as lack of parental confidence in more difficult subjects.

> Parents really want to help their child, that is why I often encounter questions during conversations at parent's evening, such as: 'What books should I purchase for my child?' or 'Do you know anyone that can tutor my child?' Therefore, I created a quiz booklet for parents to use with their children. The booklet has questions and answers for each unit. Subsequently, there is no need for parents to be experts in the subject/topic as all the answers are provided.

Development of the Plains (circa 1852-1976)

Questions	Answers
1. When did the US Civil War begin and end?	1861 to 1865
2. Who was fighting who?	Northern states vs. the Southern states
3. Give two consequences of this war.	It led many people looking to start a new life in the west, and it gave citizenship to African-American slaves.
4. What did the 1862 Homestead Act aim to do?	Settling the west with individual farmers.
5. What did the 1862 Homestead Act promise people?	Settlers could buy 160 acre plots of land for $10
6. Give one achievement of the 1862 Homestead Act.	By 1876, over six million acres of government land had already become homesteads.
7. Give one limitation of the 1862 Homestead Act.	Others bought land and then sold it for profit.
8. What did the 1862 Pacific Railroad Act lead to?	The building of the Transcontinental Railroad, which was completed in 1869.
9. What made this difficult?	Financial cost
10. Give two consequences of the transcontinental railroad.	It enabled the growth of the cattle industry, and it meant farmers could transport their crops to sell in the east.
11. How did the invention of barbed wire help the Homesteaders?	It fenced crops from animals.
12. What was the 'sulky plough'?	It was machinery used to pull up tough weeds.

Figure 7 Quiz booklet

The quiz booklet was designed to mirror the reading journal that primary students receive. Parents of Year 11 students were given this booklet at parents' evening and instructed that they had to quiz their child on a particular unit every week, then record their child's score and sign it. The following lesson, the student will complete a quiz on the same unit that their parents have quizzed them on. This saw an increase of results by an average of two marks in comparison to tests taken prior to the booklet. The booklet has knowledge questions as well as structure questions, e.g how many paragraphs do you need for a 12-mark question? What features does a 9 Grade conclusion have? Figure 8 is an example of the booklet record that students and parents have to use.

Quizzes with parents

Choose a topic and get your parent to test you on a minimum of five questions

Date	Topic	Score	Parent signature
		/	
		/	
		/	
		/	
		/	
		/	
		/	
		/	
		/	

Figure 8 Booklet record

The impact and feedback:

- A survey carried out found that student confidence increased from 12% to 62%.

- Parental confidence and interaction increased by 53% due to providing this practical resource.

- Student outcomes improved: 85% of 2019 leavers obtained grade 9-4 in comparison to my 2018 leavers who obtained 64% grade 9-4.

- Five students exceeded their target grade by more than two grades. These five students were middle ability.

- However, 31% of students commented that they preferred peer-to-peer quizzing rather than being tested by their parents.

- Students have said that they would have preferred this at the start of their GCSE course.

- Also, within the survey, students said to improve the booklet there should be more pictures to accompany difficult concepts. Therefore, going forward, I will implement more dual coding.

The booklet was trialled out in another context with Rob Hitch, Senior Vice Principal at Harris Academy South Norwood. This was his feedback:

Our Year 11 students have loved the quizzing booklets. A Year 11 student said: 'They've been brilliant, so simple to use, and they help me recall the key details I need for the exam.' The interaction it encourages between students and parents has also helped parents take a more active role in their child's learning. Some parents have commented that it has helped them understand how to ask their child the right questions. The booklets draw on the latest developments in cognitive science and represent the very best of low stakes quizzing for retrieval.

You can follow Emily on Twitter @MissFolorunsho.

Retrieval practice revision menu

The retrieval practice revision menu can be used to support revision at the end of a unit or as the exam season approaches. This menu can be easily adapted to a specific subject, topic or unit. The example I have provided is not specific to any topic or subject but I would suggest doing so. The menu provides the student with a range of different approaches linked to retrieval practice to provide variety and all tasks on the menu require retrieval. It is important that all students are familiar with all of the tasks on the menu; this can be achieved if they have completed the tasks previously, inside or outside of the lesson.

Self-test	Flash card	Past papers
Use your notes/textbook to create a quiz to self-test yourself	Create a set of flash cards with Q&A's, ready to test yourself	Complete a past exam paper and use the mark scheme to self-assess
Revision clock	**Brain dump**	**Mind map**
Break down the topic into 12 sections and complete a revision clock	Complete a brain dump with as much as you can recall then check your notes to see what you forgot	Create a mind map from memory, then check, review and add to your mind map
Infographic	**Summarise**	**Retrieve, record & review!**
Create an infographic with sketches and note from memory	Write an overview of the key topics from memory then refer back to your notes	Record yourself retrieving as much information as you can verbally then listen back and review

Figure 9 Retrieval practice revision menu

Retrieval revision bookmark

I designed this simple double-sided bookmark for my students. It was very easy to create but the most time consuming aspect can be the cutting and laminating, if you are able to delegate this or have a reprographics department then even better. Older students are very capable of cutting out and asking students to do that will take a fraction of the time it would take a teacher to do with a class set, so don't feel guilty if you do.

The idea behind this bookmark was that students would have a constant reminder of the effective study habits and some suggested methods as to how to do this. This is generic and can be used across subjects. You can directly download my template or you could adapt it to make it subject-specific or related to an exam style of question. It's a basic resource but with an important and essential message about learning that should continually be at the forefront of students' mind when revising.

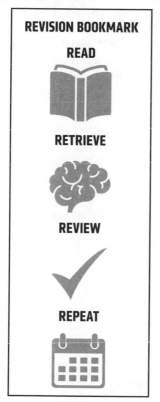
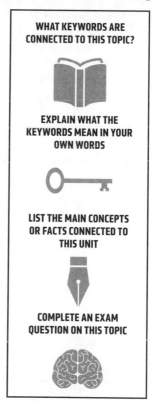

Figure 10 Retrieval revision bookmark

Effective revision habits and strategies: A guide for pupils and parents

At my previous school, the Senior Leadership Team recognised that the study guide they had previously provided for students was outdated and required an update both with its content and presentation. I volunteered to assist with this, as evidence-informed revision is an area I am really interested in and I have carried out a lot of research into this field. I also have an interest in graphic design and layout too.

I created a clear and stylish guide that was emailed to all students and parents. The revision guide briefly outlined the main principles behind retrieval practice, spaced practice, concrete examples, elaboration, interleaving, dual coding, exam vocabulary and wellbeing strategies. This booklet entitled *Effective revision habits and strategies: A study guide for pupils and parents* is available for free download.[7]

I dedicated a considerable amount of time and effort creating this resource, therefore, as shown on the following pages, I felt it should be shared with other educators, students and parents and carers as it could be of use and benefit to them too (sharing is caring). My school agreed for me to offer this resource freely. To ensure other schools could use this guide easily (without the need to edit or adapt) I removed any specific school branding. Please do download this guide and share with your colleagues, students and parents or feel free to use it as inspiration to create your own how to study guide!

---

7. There is a link in the Resources chapter.

EFFECTIVE REVISION HABITS AND STRATEGIES: A STUDY GUIDE FOR PUPILS AND PARENTS

Retrieval practice

Spaced practice

Concrete examples

Elaboration

Interleaving

Dual coding

Exam vocabulary

Wellbeing strategies and revision tools

WHAT IS RETRIEVAL PRACTICE?

'**Retrieval practice** is a learning strategy where we focus on getting information out. Through the act of retrieval, or calling information to mind, our memory for that information is strengthened and forgetting is less likely to occur. Retrieval practice is a powerful tool for improving learning.'

Use your class notes and textbooks to make a list of the important information and content that you need to know across different subjects.

Then close your books and test yourself. You can create quizzes, use flash cards or complete past exam papers. **Make sure you don't use your notes!**

Retrieve as much information as you can then check your answers. It's important to know what you know and what you don't know... yet!

Use your answers to confirm the next stage of your revision, focus on the areas that you struggled to recall from memory.

WHAT IS SPACED PRACTICE?

'Start planning early for exams and set aside a little bit of time everyday. Five hours spread out over two weeks is better than the same five hours all at once.' This is **space practice** and it is regarded as one of the most effective revision strategies.

Divide up your revision into short manageable chunks of time. When revising aim for 20-30 minutes per session.

Mass practice or cramming is not effective and can be stressful. This is when you study for a very intense period of time just before the exam.

You need to plan your time carefully to ensure all subjects and topics are covered in shorter chunks over a longer period of time.

Dividing up your revision into smaller, manageable sections will benefit you in the long-term; the revision you do for mocks will stick for the final exams.

WHAT IS DUAL CODING?

'**Dual coding** is the process of combining verbal materials with visual materials. There are many ways to visually represent materials, such as with infographics, timelines, cartoon/comic strips, diagrams and graphic organisers.'

Dual coding involves you the learner drawing images, graphs, diagrams or timelines to support your revision notes.

When you are revising using your class materials find or create visuals that link with the information. Compare and combine the visuals with the words.

Don't worry if you don't consider yourself an artist – it isn't about the quality of your illustrations, the focus is to improve and deepen your understanding.

Make sure your images/diagrams are relevant. Be careful when using photos as too many background images can detract from the main points.

WELLBEING DURING EXAMS

The exam period can be stressful that is why it's very important that you revise and prepare as this can help to reduce exam anxiety. In addition to revising there are other strategies you can do to look after your **mental and physical health**.

Eat. Diet is important so don't neglect it during the exam period. Don't skip meals, stay consistent with a healthy balance of meals and stay hydrated.

Sleep. Staying up late to revise is a bad idea! Sleep deprivation can have a very negative impact on concentration, performance and memory.

Exercise. Take regular breaks from revision with exercise. Take part in a sport you enjoy, go for a walk or any activity that is active and part of your daily routine.

Relax. Relax during the exam period? Yes! It is essential that you do make time to switch off and have a break. Watch Netflix, read or talk to your friends.

WHAT IS ELABORATION?

'The term **elaboration** can be used to mean a lot of different things. However, when we are talking about studying using elaboration, it involves explaining and describing ideas with detail. Elaboration also involves making connections among ideas you are trying to learn.'

Elaboration involves asking further questions and making links to help you connect new information with what you already know.

Ask yourself questions about a topic to delve deeper. The more information you have about a specific topic the stronger your grasp and ability to recall.

When you learn about the causes of WW1, you could which causes are linked together? Which causes are short or long-term? What was the major cause?

Another way to elaborate is to take two ideas or concepts and think about the various ways they are similar and how they are different.

WHAT IS INTERLEAVING?

'**Interleaving** is a process where students mix and combine multiple subjects and topics while they study in order to improve their learning. Blocked practice on the other hand, involves studying one topic very thoroughly before moving to another. Interleaving has been shown to more effective than blocked practice leading to better long-term retention.'

Monday	Tuesday	Wednesday	Thursday	Friday
Algebra	Ratio	Statistics	Ratio	Algebra
Geometry	Statistics	Algebra	Geometry	Statistics

REFERENCES

www.retrievalpractice.org

www.learningscientists.org

Wellington College (2018) '5 Habits of an Effective Learner', *Wellington College* [Online]. Retrieved from: www.bit.ly/2qIYHSM

University of Arizona (no date) 'Interleaving: A Strategy in the Learning to Learn Series', *University of Arizona* [Online], Retrieved from: www.bit.ly/2WDuDyg

McDaniel, M. A., Brown, P. C. and Roediger, H. L. (2014) *Make It Stick: The Science of Successful Learning*. Cambridge, MA: Harvard University Press.

Dunlosky, J. (2013) 'Strengthening the Student Toolbox: Study Strategies to Boost Learning', *American Educator* 37 (3) pp. 12-21. Retrieved from: www.bit.ly/33eJTEn

As I have mentioned throughout this book, I feel very fortunate and grateful to be working at a school that promotes and supports teachers to become research and evidence informed. My colleague and Deputy Headteacher at BSAK James McBlane created a document to support teachers with this process. James made a comparison of the process of engaging with research to a real life example and common scenario.

James suggested thinking about the process you might go through if you set yourself the goal of leading a healthier and more active lifestyle. You have self-evaluated and decided that you can improve, perhaps the goal is to lose weight or become fitter or both. Where do you start?

It is likely that you would do some research on healthy eating, you might read some online articles, you may purchase a book or two in order to find out more and inform your decisions. You might also start 'researching' exercise options. Another option you might decide on is to talk to people you know who have already achieved this to find out what they do and what works for them. You may even use social media as a way to learn from others or gain inspiration. You may also research exercise classes in your local gym and consider how these might meet your individual needs. This is research. If you follow through you would start to use this information to make some changes in your behaviour. You might stop ordering takeaways and plan healthy shopping lists and meals, you might decide to up-skill yourself by taking a cooking course or buying a healthy cookbook and self-learning.

Over time, you would evaluate your progress, you might quantifiably measure progress on the scales or you might qualitatively evaluate how you feel, noticing you feel better in yourself and have more energy. What you have just done is take an evidence-based and research-informed approach to your personal development to support the goal you set yourself. In essence this is all we mean when we talk about an evidence-based and research-informed approach to professional learning.

I like this analogy so much, I decided to take it even further.

When thinking about getting fitter and healthier it is tempting to seek out quick-win solutions that will shed the pounds fast and have a visible impact for you and others to see. We all know that to become healthy requires permanent changes to lifestyle that are sustainable and simply do not happen overnight. Yet, despite this, many people resort to unhealthy and extreme weight loss solutions, supplements and plans. These healthy strategies often claim to be supported by research, but is that research credible, reliable or accurate? When researching and learning about health and fitness there is a vast amount of content available so we have to be careful, selective and cautious about what we read and decide to act on. There is no silver bullet when it comes to our health.

In regards to education, there have been many fads, gimmicks, tools and ideas that have been sold and marketed as the solution to improving exam results, a method of achieving outstanding inspection reports or transform schools in a radical, yet miraculous, way. A lot of time and money has been invested in these attempts over the years. There have been claims made in the name of academic research but are actually neuromyths that, unfortunately, continue to stand the test of time. Just like a healthy mind and body learning takes place over the long-term, there is no quick-win or short-term answer. Losing weight and maintaining a healthy routine is often hard, challenging and difficult. Learning is often hard, challenging and difficult. There is no silver bullet when it comes to education.

Just like a one-off salad won't change your physique, a one-off retrieval quiz won't guarantee information can be retrieved from long-term memory. Retrieval practice, like exercise, must be consistent, regular and the level of challenge should be appropriate with desirable difficulties. A salad alone doesn't make up a balanced healthy diet in the same sense that retrieval practice shouldn't be used as the only strategy to support teaching and learning.

No doubt our knowledge and understanding of retrieval practice will continue to evolve and further develop. We can hope that future teachers will not be misled with neuromyths but instead be equipped with the knowledge and understanding that we have about effective teaching and learning strategies. As for experienced teachers we can continue to combine educational research with our own reflections and experiences, which is the ultimate combination when it comes to supporting our students learning.

Summary

- Retrieval practice should not been regarded as simply a revision strategy but instead a learning strategy that should be used throughout the academic year, not just the exam season.

- Retrieval practice is one ingredient in the recipe for success. It must be combined with spaced practice and other factors are of equal value and importance, including attendance, support, motivation, attitude and so on.

- There is now a new generation of young people embracing revision strategies, the Study Tubers. They are blogging and vlogging about how to revise and deal with exam stress. This is great but we still need to educate our students about the science of learning.

- In addition to informing our students about these strategies, we should aim to spread the knowledge with parents and carers too.

Recommended reading

Teach Like Nobody's Watching: The essential guide to effective and efficient teaching by Mark Enser

The Truth About Teaching: An Evidence-Informed Guide for New Teachers by Greg Ashman

Exam Literacy: A guide to doing what works (and not what does not) to better prepare students for exams by Jake Hunton

The Confident Teacher: Developing successful habits of mind, body and pedagogy by Alex Quigley

How We Learn: The Surprising Truth About When, Where and Why It Happens by Benedict Carey

RESOURCES

You scan the QR codes below to be instantly directed to websites where you can download resource templates shown in this book for free.

 My TES resources homepage

 My educational website and blog

 ICTEvangelist.com – Download Retrieval Practice Challenge Grid templates

 Pete Sanderson's Snakes and Ladders template

 A glossary of learning terms by James Mannion

 Revision clock template